Cyprus

DIAMOND BOOKS

The blue section answers the question 'I would like to see or do something; where do I go and what do I see when I get there?' This section is arranged as an alphabetical list of topics. Within each topic you will find:

- A selection of the best examples on offer.
- How to get there, costs and opening hours for each entry.
- The outstanding features of each entry.
- A simplified map, with each entry plotted and the nearest landmark or transport access.

The red section is a lively and informative gazetteer. It offers:
- Essential facts about the main places and cultural items.
  What is La Bastille? Who was Michelangelo? Where is Delphi?

The gold section is full of practical and invaluable travel information. It offers:
- Everything you need to know to help you enjoy yourself and get the most out of your time away, from Accommodation through Baby-sitters, Car Hire, Food, Health, Money, Newspapers, Taxis, Telephones to Youth Hostels.

Cross-references:

Type in small capitals – CHURCHES – tells you that more information on an item is available within the topic on churches.

A-Z after an item tells you that more information is available within the gazetteer. Simply look under the appropriate name.

A name in bold – **Holy Cathedral** – also tells you that more information on an item is available in the gazetteer – again simply look up the name.

CONTENTS

■ **CULTURAL/HISTORICAL GAZETTEER**

CONTENTS

■ PRACTICAL INFORMATION GAZETTEER

Lachi

INTRODUCTION

The third-largest and most easterly Mediterranean island, Cyprus lies 65 km south of Turkey and 130 km west of Syria, and has a population of 670,000, of which 77.1% are Greek, 18.1% are Turks (almost all living in the Turkish-occupied sector) and 4.8% are from other minorities. Some 225 km from east to west and 95 km north to south, with a land area less than half that of Wales, Cyprus offers a stunning range of landscapes from the dusty eastern plain of the Mesaoria to the pine-clad slopes of the Troodos mountains. The coastline is studded with some of the finest beaches in the Mediterranean with relatively unpolluted seas, while for the historically-minded the island is scattered with the remains of its turbulent history.

The island is dominated by two mountain ranges: a narrow limestone spine running east to west across the northern part of the island, rising to over 915 m and known as Pentadaktylos (Greek for 'five fingers'); and the Troodos range, a massif of volcanic origin rising to 1950 m, occupying much of the west of the island. The plain of the Mesaoria, lying between these ranges, is a fertile agricultural area dotted with farming villages relying on the production of grain for their livelihood. The mainstay of the Cyprus economy has traditionally been agriculture and agriculture-based enterprises such as canning and vineries, although light manufacturing and tourism in particular are increasingly important. The centre of the wine industry is the southern port of Limassol and vines can be seen growing in the limestone foothills around the town and stretching along the coast to the ancient city of Paphos in the west. Limassol is also important for citrus fruit.

While the sun-soaked beaches will be sufficient attraction for many, the picturesque villages and monasteries of the Troodos mountains are well worth visiting. Country roads wind breathtakingly, cut into the hillside, offering spectacular views across deep forests to the sea beyond, and the cool mountain air is wonderfully refreshing after the blistering summer heat of the coast. However, Troodos has not only offered Cypriots a refuge from the summer heat as it still does today but in past times it was a haven safe from marauders and raiders who frequently preyed on the coastal towns, and consequently the mountain monasteries contain a rich collection of the island's Byzantine cultural heritage. Arguably the most important of these is Kykkos, the largest monastery in Cyprus

Lefkara

and founded in the 12thC, but others worth visiting are Trooditissa and Omodhos, as well as Assinou church with its fine frescoes. However, the most spectacularly-situated of the Cyprus monasteries, Stavrovouni, lies not in Troodos but perched precariously at the top of a volcanic stack 700 m high which towers above the surrounding countryside. The ascent is not for those without a head for heights but those who do brave the numerous hairpin bends are rewarded with an unsurpassed view across to the southeastern port of Larnaca.

Larnaca, in Ottoman times the main port of the island, is known among ornithologists for its salt lake that provides a habitat for numerous species of birds, including migratory flamingos, in the winter months. Indeed, the whole island being on many migration routes is of special interest to the bird-watcher. Although the summer visitor looking at the parched land may find it hard to appreciate, Cyprus in spring is also a paradise for the botanist when the countryside is ablaze with wild flowers, some of which are unique to the island.

Those with an interest in the past will not be disappointed with Cyprus. Owing to its strategic position Cyprus has been conquered and fought over innumerable times in the course of its long history. The settlement at Khirokitia between Limassol and Larnaca, dating back to 6800 BC, is one of the earliest Neolithic cultures in the world. Cyprus, however, came into its own during the Chalcolithic (3900 BC-2500 BC) and Bronze (2500 BC-1050 BC) ages, being a major source of copper ore; indeed our word 'copper' comes, via the Latin, from the Greek name of the island, Kypros. It was during the Bronze Age that the island was colonized by Greeks, first from about 1400 BC by Mycenaeans and later in the 12th and 11thC BC by Achaeans. Remains of Mycenaean buildings can be seen at the ancient city of Kition, modern Larnaca. The first millennium BC saw the island falling under the control of Phoenicians, Assyrians, Egyptians and Persians, the latter being expelled when the island became part of the empire of Alexander the Great in 333 BC. The Greek culture that had developed on the island largely untouched by mainland developments (for example, syllabic scripts related to those found at Mycenaean sites in Greece dating from the 14thC BC were in use in Cyprus as late as the 4thC BC) now came within the mainstream Hellenistic influences. Paphos became the capital and this period saw the rise of many important cities such as Curium, west of modern Limassol. In 58 BC Cyprus became part of the Roman Empire and some hundred years later was to play an important role in the spread of Christianity when in AD 45 the

island was converted by saints Paul and Barnabas. After the move of the imperial capital to Constantinople in AD 330 and the subsequent division of the Roman Empire, Cyprus became part of the Eastern Empire that evolved into the Byzantine Empire. Invaded by Arabs in 647, the island for three centuries remained on the front line in the battle between Byzantium and Islam, until the expulsion of the Arabs from Asia Minor and Cyprus by the Byzantine emperor Nikiphoros Phocas in 963. In 1191 Richard I of England (Richard the Lionheart) was shipwrecked on Cyprus and claiming rudeness on the part of the unpopular governor, Isaac Comnenos, took possession of the island, later selling it to the Knights Templars who in turn in 1192 sold it on to Guy de Lusignan, thus beginning a period of almost 300 years of Frankish rule. It is during this period that Nicosia became capital of the island and many fine examples of medieval architecture were erected. The last of the Lusignan rulers, Queen Catherine Cornaro, bequeathed the island to the Venetians, who were responsible for the massive fortifications still visible around the old cities of Nicosia and Famagusta (the latter the setting of Shakespeare's play, *Othello*). Despite their size and ingenuity these did not prevent the island, its Greek population demoralized from

Cape Drepanum

Venetian oppression, falling to the Ottoman Turks in 1571. The years of Turkish occupation saw the island, isolated from Western influences, decline in importance, suffering from maladministration and neglect, and the population, smitten by poverty and disease, suffered a significant reduction in numbers.

The weakening of the Ottoman Empire and the sudden rise in strategic importance of Cyprus on the completion of the Suez canal in 1869 were to change its history. The British leased Cyprus from Turkey in 1878, later to annex it on the outbreak of war in 1914, the island finally becoming a crown colony under the Treaty of Lausanne in 1923. The Cypriots, having suffered to varying degrees for centuries under Lusignan, Venetian and Turkish rule, initially saw British occupation as their salvation, believing that after a short period under British rule the island would be reunited with mainland Greece as had been the case with the Ionian Islands. When this did not occur armed insurrection finally broke out in 1955, with a bitter terrorist campaign that lasted until a compromise solution was worked out, giving the island independence (rather than the initial objective of union with Greece) in 1960. After independence, despite intercommunal disputes over the

complex constitution, sometimes resulting in violence, which led to UN peacekeeping forces being despatched to the island in 1964 – where they remain to this day – the Cyprus economy prospered. However, in 1974 the Athens dictatorship sponsored a coup against the Cyprus government with the aim of bringing about union; this resulted in Turkish forces invading the northern part of the island and also led to the dictatorship's own downfall. The immediate post-1974 situation continues today with 37% of Cyprus territory under Turkish occupation, no solution having yet been found.

Despite the sombre political background there is no reason why the traveller cannot enjoy the many delights Cyprus has to offer. The Cypriots are a friendly people and are anxious that the visitor enjoys his stay. Facilities for the tourist are generally of a high standard with hotels ranging from the simple to some of the best in Europe, and restaurants cover a range of cuisines from Chinese to Lebanese, although most visitors will find the local dishes of grilled meats and fish, fresh salad and locally-picked fruit, washed down with the excellent local beer or wine, the ideal way to relax, whether after lazing on the beach or after a strenuous hike through the mountains.

Skarinou

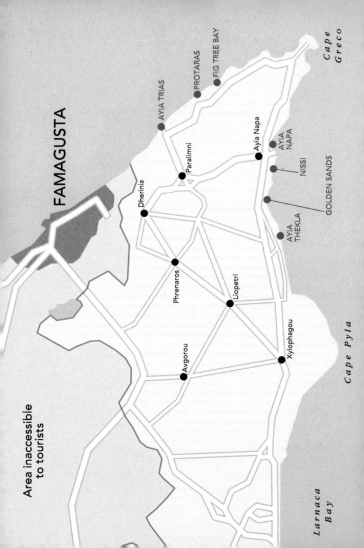

FAMAGUSTA

Area inaccessible to tourists

Cape Greco

FIG TREE BAY

PROTARAS

AYIA TRIAS

Paralimni

Ayia Napa

AYIA NAPA

NISSI

GOLDEN SANDS

Dherinia

AYIA THEKLA

Phrenaros

Liopetri

Xylophagou

Avgorou

Cape Pyla

Larnaca Bay

Beaches

*Few would deny that the Ayia Napa area contains the best sandy
beaches on Cyprus. Indeed, the whole coastline from Dhekelia in the
west to the Green Line (see A-Z) in the north is a series of shallow,
mainly sandy, bays, with the exception of the cliffs round Cape Greco.
Owing to the attraction of these beaches, Ayia Napa itself has seen
considerable tourist development in recent years. However, some of the
outlying beaches, easily reached by car or bicycle, are less crowded,
though water-sport facilities are liable to be less in evidence.*

AYIA TRIAS 19 km northeast of Ayia Napa. Car.
*Small sandy bay. Some water sports. Good taverna. Relatively quiet and
undeveloped. See* AYIA NAPA-EXCURSION.

PROTARAS 16 km northeast of Ayia Napa. Car.
Good sandy beach. Full range of water sports. Tavernas. See AYIA NAPA-
EXCURSION, A-Z.

FIG TREE BAY
15 km northeast of Ayia Napa to the south of Protaras (see above). Car.
Sandy sheltered beach. Taverna and water sports. See AYIA NAPA-
EXCURSION, A-Z.

AYIA NAPA (MAIN BEACH)
*Extensive sandy beach. All manner of water sports, tavernas, cafés, etc.
Can get crowded in high season. There is a small, picturesque fishing
harbour at the west end of the beach, a reminder of Ayia Napa's
principal source of income 20 years ago. See* A-Z.

NISSI 3 km west of Ayia Napa. Car, foot, bicycle.
Sandy bay. Tavernas, water sports. Popular.

GOLDEN SANDS 4 km west of Ayia Napa. Car, bicycle.
Isthmus with sandy beaches both sides. Water sports, tavernas.

AYIA THEKLA 7 km west of Ayia Napa. Car, bicycle.
Sandy bay. Few facilities other than an ice-cream van.

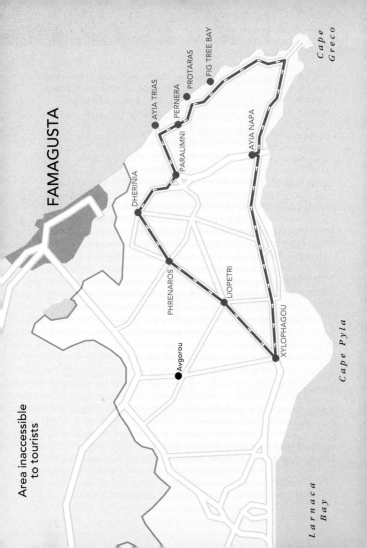

Excursion

53 km. A half-day excursion covering the southeastern corner of Cyprus, noted for its potato production as well as its excellent beaches. Although the route contains a few gradients, this part of Cyprus is relatively flat and the excursion could therefore be made by bicycle.

Leaving the town of Ayia Napa, turn right onto the main road in the direction of Cape Greco.

6 km – Cape Greco. The southeastern tip of Cyprus. The cape itself, with its radio aerials and lighthouse, is not accessible, the main road skirting it about 0.5 km to the northwest. Past the cape the road turns through 90° to the north and the beaches lying along the coast to the right-hand side of the road are some of the best sandy beaches in Cyprus, notably Fig Tree Bay and Protaras (see **AYIA NAPA-BEACHES**). Not surprisingly there is considerable tourist development in this area. North of Pernera the road turns inland (a detour of 1 km can be made by taking the right-hand fork to the little bay of Ayia Trias (see **AYIA NAPA-BEACHES**).

20 km – Paralimni. Once largely dependent on agriculture for their income, the residents of Paralimni have greatly benefited from revenue from tourism which is reflected in the amount of new building in the village. Paralimni is also a traditional centre for delicacies such as pieces of smoked pork (*pastá*) and pork sausage (*lookánika*). Follow the signs for Dherinia.

24 km – Dherinia. Take a short detour to the northern edge of the village where you will meet the boundary with the part of the island occupied by the Turkish army (see **Green Line**). You should note that photography in this region is forbidden. From here you will be able to see the abandoned hotels of the occupied city of Famagusta in the distance. Returning to the centre of the village, take the road leading to Phrenaros, then continue to Liopetri and Xylophagou. The rich red soils in this region support intensive horticulture and the area is noted for its potatoes in particular.

39 km – Xylophagou. Turn left onto the main road, reaching Ayia Napa after 14 km.

Nightlife

VIP Makarios III Avenue.
On main road leading from town to seafront. ● Moderate.
Disco and nightspot.

BABYLON Ayias Mavris Street.
Behind Seferis Square. ● Moderate.
Disco and nightclub; popular with a young clientele.

BLUE LAGOON Protaras.
12 km east along coast from Ayia Napa. ● Moderate.
Disco.

P'ZAZZ Kryou Nerou Avenue.
Almost opposite Grecian Bay Hotel. ● Moderate.
Popular disco.

APOCALYPSE Kryou Nerou Avenue.
Along coast road a little out of town centre. ● Moderate.
Disco on ground floor and bouzouki music on first floor.

STRINGFELLOWS Nissi Avenue.
West of town centre along coast road. ● Moderate.
Lively disco.

LP'S Nissi Avenue.
West of town centre along coast road. ● Moderate.
Nightclub and disco.

BLACK & WHITE Ippocratous Street.
Centrally located just off Seferis Square. ● Moderate.
Disco and nightclub.

KAHLUA PUB Ayias Mavris Street.
Behind Seferis Square. ● Moderate.
Exotic cocktails mainly served to a younger clientele.

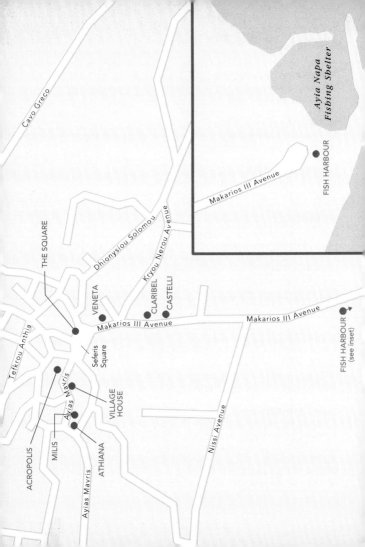

Restaurants

VENETA Makarios III Avenue. Opposite monastery.
▨ All day. ● Moderate.
Steaks, pizzas and seafood.

CLARIBEL Makarios III Avenue.
▨ Dinner. ● Moderate.
Cyprus and international cuisine. Roof garden.

CASTELLI Makarios III Avenue.
▨ Lunch and dinner. ● Moderate.
Cyprus and international cuisine. Children's menu.

ACROPOLIS 20 Katalimata Street. Behind monastery.
▨ Dinner. ● Moderate.
Grills and Cyprus specialities (souvlákia, suckling pig). Good view.

VILLAGE HOUSE Ayias Mavris Street.
▨ Dinner. ● Moderate.
Cyprus dishes and steaks.

FISH HARBOUR Limanaki. By old fishing shelter.
▨ Lunch and dinner. ● Moderate.
Fresh fish. Remember that in Cyprus fish is expensive compared to meat.

ATHIANA 10 Ayias Mavris Street.
▨ Lunch and dinner. ● Moderate.
Mainly grills and Cyprus dishes although some international cooking.

THE SQUARE Seferis Square.
▨ All day. ● Inexpensive.
Pub and café serving pizzas, burgers, toasted sandwiches, alcoholic and non-alcoholic drinks and ice creams.

MILIS Ayias Mavris Street.
▨ All day. ● Inexpensive.
Charcoal grills, soups, salads and pasta dishes.

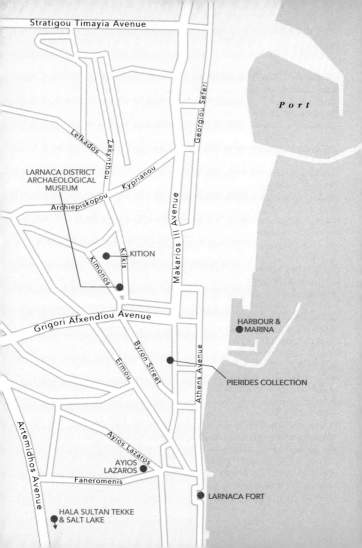

Stratigou Timayia Avenue

Lefkados

Zakynthou

Kyprianou

Georgiou Seferi

Port

LARNACA DISTRICT
ARCHAEOLOGICAL
MUSEUM

Archiepiskopou

Kilkis

KITION

Kimonos

Makarios III Avenue

Grigori Afxendiou Avenue

Ermou

Byron Street

Athens Avenue

HARBOUR &
MARINA

PIERIDES COLLECTION

Artemidhos Avenue

Ayios Lazaros

AYIOS
LAZAROS

Faneromenis

LARNACA FORT

HALA SULTAN TEKKE
& SALT LAKE

LARNACA DISTRICT ARCHAEOLOGICAL MUSEUM

Kalograion Square. North of main shopping area. ■ Summer: 0730-1330
Mon.-Sat.; Winter: 0730-1400 Mon.-Fri., 0730-1300 Sat. ● £C0.50.
Archaeological collection of artefacts found in the Larnaca district, in
particular from the site of Kition (see below).

PIERIDES COLLECTION Swedish Consulate, Zenon Kitieos Street.
■ 0900-1300 Mon.-Sat. ● £C0.50.
Amassed privately by the Pierides family, this is one of the finest collec-
tions of Cyprus antiquities outside the Cyprus Museum (see NICOSIA-
ATTRACTIONS 1*) and covers the period from Neolithic to Byzantine times.*
Currently housed in the Swedish Consulate, this important collection is
due to move to a new home, so it would be best to check locally.

KITION Off Archiepiskopou Kyprianou, north of Larnaca District
Archaeological Museum. ■ Summer: 0730-1330 Mon.-Sat.; Winter:
0730-1400 Mon.-Fri., 0730-1300 Sat. ● £C0.50.
The acropolis of the ancient city of Kition (13thC BC) is currently under
excavation. Other areas of Kition are being excavated in other parts of
Larnaca but are of little interest except to the professional archaeologist.
See **Larnaca**.

LARNACA FORT South of town and north of old Turkish quarter.
■ Summer: 0730-1930 Mon.-Sat.; Winter: 0730-sunset Mon.-Sat.
● £C0.50.
Built by the Turks in 1625 and now housing a few finds from Kition (see
above) as well as objects from Hala Sultan Tekke (see LARNACA-ATTRAC-
TIONS 2*). Good views of the seafront are to be had from the sea wall.*

AYIOS LAZAROS Ayios Lazaros Street.
Church originally erected in the 9thC (later rebuilt) over the tomb of
Lazarus (the same Lazarus who was raised from the dead by Christ and
later settled in Larnaca). The empty tomb still exists, the body being sent
to Constantinople at the time of the original discovery of the tomb. Steps
lead down from the right of the iconostasis (screen with tiered icons) to
the crypt containing the tomb.

Hala Sultan Tekke

Attractions 2

HARBOUR & MARINA Athens Avenue.
The picturesque harbour and marina with its promenade, the Finikoudes, named after the tall palm trees that line it, is a well-known landmark of Larnaca and a popular place for an evening stroll for both visitors and residents.

HALA SULTAN TEKKE & SALT LAKE
3 km west of Larnaca take right turn just past airport.
*Situated on the shores of Larnaca salt lake (see **A-Z**), the Hala Sultan Tekke mosque, built in 1816 (though parts are much older), lies over the tomb of Umm Haram, aunt of the Prophet Mohammed, who died during the first Arab raid on Cyprus. It is an important place of pilgrimage for Muslims. See **LARNACA-EXCURSION 2**.*

Avdhellero

Pyla

Oroklini

LARNACA
PUBLIC BEACH

Aradhippou

SANDY BEACH
HOTEL AREA

BEACHES NORTH OF LARNACA

*Larnaca
Bay*

FINIKOUDES

LARNACA

*Salt
Lake*

MACKENZIE

Meneou

Kiti

KITI

Perivolia   PHAROS   *Cape
Kiti*

*Mediterranean
Sea*

Beaches

LARNACA PUBLIC BEACH
10 km northeast of Larnaca. Bus, car.
*Sandy beach. Restaurant, café and changing facilities. Water sports. Car park. Run by the Cyprus Tourism Organization (see **A-Z**).*

SANDY BEACH HOTEL AREA 8 km northeast. Bus, car.
Pleasant sandy beaches, some sheltered by offshore moles. Good for children. Good selection of water sports. Refreshments and meals can be obtained from hotels. NOTE: If you use hotel facilities such as sun beds you will be expected to pay for them.

BEACHES NORTH OF LARNACA
3-6 km north of Larnaca. Bus, car.
A number of beaches, many sandy, frequented mainly by Cypriots. However, enjoyment of these is marred by the smell of the oil refinery that lies just north of the town.

FINIKOUDES (TOWN BEACH) Running along Athens Avenue.
*More enjoyable for the promenade of palms (Finikoudes) than the beach itself where the sand seems to have become compacted by the constant crowds. Extensive range of water sports. Cafés and restaurants of all types line the promenade (see **LARNACA-RESTAURANTS**).*

MACKENZIE (TOWN BEACH)
South of town past fishing shelter on Piyale Pasha St. Bus, car.
Mainly sandy small beaches. Popular with locals and can be very crowded at weekends. Water sports, many restaurants and cafés.

KITI 10 km south of Larnaca. Car.
Pebbly and rocky with some areas of sand. No facilities other than an isolated taverna.

PHAROS 18 km south of Larnaca. Car.
Rather exposed pebbly beach. Development underway but at present few facilities other than a couple of cafés. Additional facilities are available at the two hotels on Cape Kiti itself.

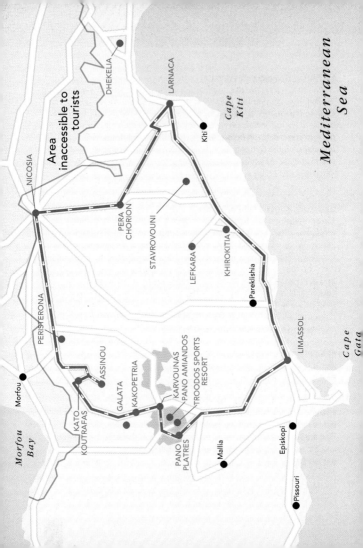

Mediterranean
Sea

*Area
inaccessible to
tourists*

DHEKELIA

LARNACA

*Cape
Kiti*

Kiti

NICOSIA

PERA
CHORION

STAVROVOUNI

LEFKARA

KHIROKITIA

Pareklishia

LIMASSOL

*Cape
Gata*

PERISTERONA

ASSINOU

KATO
KOUTRAFAS

GALATA

KAKOPETRIA

KARVOUNAS
PANO AMIANDOS
TROODOS SPORTS
RESORT

PANO
PLATRES

Mallia

Episkopi

Pissouri

*Morfou
Bay*

Morfou

Excursion 1

*237 km. A two-day excursion to the Troodos mountains via Nicosia.
Although it is possible to complete this excursion in one day, two days
are required to complete the side trips and to allow sufficient time to
explore the villages en route. An overnight stop at the mountain resorts
of either Platres or Kakopetria is recommended, though it is advisable to
book accommodation before setting out since these resorts are very
popular with the Cypriots in summer. This excursion can also be started
from Limassol, in which case you should take the Nicosia motorway and
join the route 21 km south of Nicosia.*

Take the recently completed motorway (not marked on all maps) out of
Larnaca in the direction of Nicosia. If you are staying in one of the
many hotels on the coast north of Larnaca you can avoid driving
through the town centre by taking the coast road in the direction of
Dhekelia (i.e. away from Larnaca!). Immediately after the entrance to
Larnaca Public Beach (see **LARNACA-BEACHES**) turn left at the traffic lights
onto the ring road which will take you onto the motorway.
26 km – Pera Chorion. After climbing gently through arid hilly
countryside the motorway meets the Limassol–Nicosia motorway.
Continuing in the direction of Nicosia the motorway descends to the
western part of the central plain, the Mesaoria, and the Pentadaktylos
mountains will be seen in the distance. The road enters the city past the
Cyprus Broadcasting Corporation, the police headquarters and the
Hilton Hotel to meet the eastern end of Archbishop Makarios III
Avenue, one of the main shopping thoroughfares.
47 km – Nicosia (see **A-Z**). A good chance for some sightseeing (see
NICOSIA-ATTRACTIONS 1 & 2) or just a stop for coffee. However, if you are
travelling during summer remember when planning your trip that
Nicosia can get far hotter than the coast during the day with shade
temperatures sometimes exceeding 40°C. Following the signs for
Troodos, leave Nicosia to the southwest through the suburbs of Engomi
and Strovolos, bypassing Nicosia International Airport, disused since
the Turkish invasion of 1974, and rejoin the pre-1974 Nicosia–Troodos
road at the village of Kokkinotrimithia.
82 km – Peristerona. The main road skirts the village of Peristerona to
the north but it is well worth making the small detour into the village to

see the five-domed church of Saints Barnabas and Hilarion, the interior of which contains a 16thC iconostasis (screen with icons). Returning to the main road, you can take a left turn after 8 km to visit Assinou church.

90 km – Assinou. If you have time it is worth making this detour (21 km) to visit the 12thC Assinou church which contains some of the finest Byzantine murals on Cyprus. After leaving the main road you will need to stop at the village of Nikitari to find the priest who has the key to the church (try the café opposite the church in Nikitari). You can rejoin the main road through the villages of Pano and Kato Koutrafas.

113 km – Kakopetria (see **A-Z**). A popular hill resort and a good base for exploring the surrounding countryside. If you have time and energy left the churches of Ayios Sozomenos or Podithou monastery in nearby Galata (see **A-Z**) are worth visiting, or alternatively you may just wish to relax over a meal of locally farmed trout. The road climbs upwards to the Karvounas crossroads where you should take the right-hand turning in the direction of Troodos.

125 km – Troodos (see **A-Z**). After passing the massive opencast asbestos workings (no longer in operation) at Pano Amiandos you reach the sports resort of Troodos. A short detour (6 km) will take you to the summit of Mount Olympus, the highest point in Cyprus (1950 m). Returning to the square at Troodos, take the Platres turning, after which the road winds down the mountainside giving excellent views.

132 km – Pano Platres (see **LIMASSOL-EXCURSION 2**). An important hill resort with good views over the south of the Troodos range, and a popular summer resort of Cypriots themselves, meaning that accommodation tends to be heavily booked. Those seeking respite from their car may be tempted to make the relatively short walk to the

Caledonian falls (a track leads from the main road northeast of the town centre). From Platres continue on the main road following the signs to Limassol.

173 km – Limassol (see **A-Z**). The second city of Cyprus and the island's main port. You may wish to sightsee (see **LIMASSOL-ATTRACTIONS**) or merely do some shopping in the busy commercial area by the seafront (partially pedestrianized). However, if you wish to avoid Limassol itself you can turn left onto the Nicosia motorway some 2 km outside the city.

211 km – Khirokitia (see **A-Z**). Take the turning off the motorway (signposted) to visit this Neolithic site dating from about 7000–6000 BC. A further detour can be made here to the 'lace'-making village of Lefkara (see **A-Z**), about 12 km west of the motorway. After rejoining the motorway take the Larnaca junction a little further to the north which, passing south of the monastery of Stavrovouni (see **A-Z**), will bring you back to Larnaca, a distance of 26 km.

Limassol

Excursion 2

31 km. A half-day excursion taking in two of the most interesting buildings in Cyprus, the Hala Sultan Tekke on the Larnaca salt lake and Kiti church with its exceptional Byzantine mosaics.

Leave Larnaca to the south following the airport road. Passing the salt lake (see **A-Z**) on your right and continuing for about 1 km past the roundabout from which the approach road to the airport bears off, you will reach a minor road on your right signposted to the Hala Sultan Tekke. This track continues along the shore of the salt lake for about 1 km. If you are making this excursion during the winter months you may be fortunate and see flocks of migrating flamingos.

6 km – Hala Sultan Tekke (see **LARNACA-ATTRACTIONS 2**). More remarkable for its setting than its architecture this small mosque is the burial place of Umm Haram, the aunt of the Prophet Mohammed. When entering the mosque shoes should be left by the door. Returning to the main road, turn right in the direction of Kiti.

12 km – Kiti. An effort should be made to visit the impressive church of Panayia Angeloktistos, which means 'built by the angels'. If the church is not open try asking at neighbouring houses for the key. The church, built on the site of an earlier basilica, dates from around 1000 BC, having been restored in the 16thC. The date of the Byzantine mosaic showing the Virgin and Child between the archangels Michael and Gabriel is disputed but thought to be between the 5th and 9thC. It is the finest example of its type on the island and arguably one of the finest of all Byzantine mosaics, even rivalling those in Ravenna, Italy. If time is limited or the weather poor, your return journey to Larnaca should follow the outward route. However, for greater variety take the road leading from Kiti village via Perivolia to Cape Kiti.

16 km – Cape Kiti. Tourism is just beginning to reach this formerly somewhat remote region. The elevation of the cape itself offers good views over Larnaca Bay and there are a couple of hotels for refreshments. A track, rather rough in parts (although negotiable with care without the need of a four-wheel drive vehicle), runs north parallel to the narrow stony beach (see **LARNACA-BEACHES**), finally turning inland to meet the main road at Meneou, where a right turn will take you back to Larnaca, a distance of 15 km from Cape Kiti.

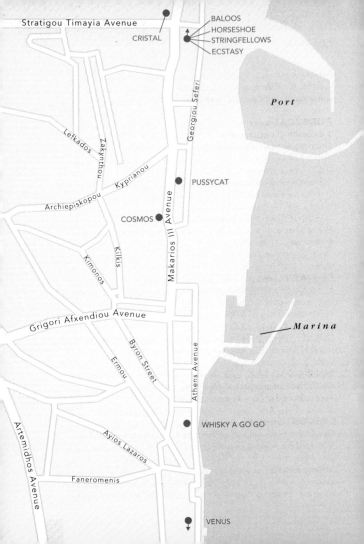

Stratigou Timayia Avenue

CRISTAL

BALOOS
HORSESHOE
STRINGFELLOWS
ECSTASY

Port

Lefkados

Zakynthou

Archiepiskopou

Kyprianou

Georgiou Seferi

Makarios III Avenue

PUSSYCAT

COSMOS

Kilkis

Kimonos

Grigori Afxendiou Avenue

Byron Street

Ermou

Athens Avenue

Marina

Artemidhos Avenue

Ayios Lazaros

WHISKY A GO GO

Faneromenis

VENUS

VENUS Mackenzie Beach.
1 km south of town centre on seafront. ● Expensive.
International and bouzouki music. Floor show.

PUSSYCAT Makarios III Avenue.
1 km north of town centre on Dhekelia road. ● Moderate.
Disco music and light show.

CRISTAL Port Roundabout, Makarios III Avenue.
1.5 km north of town centre on Dhekelia road. ● Moderate.
Dancing and cocktails.

STRINGFELLOWS Larnaca–Dhekelia road.
About 5 km north of town centre near Karpasiana Beach Hotel.
● Moderate.
Disco dancing and laser light show.

ECSTASY Larnaca–Dhekelia road.
About 6 km north of town centre beyond Stringfellows. ● Moderate.
Disco dancing. Also live music.

WHISKY A GO GO Athens Avenue.
Larnaca seafront opposite promenade (Finikoudes). ● Moderate.
Disco in popular and lively area.

COSMOS 37a Makarios III Avenue.
Just north of town centre. ● Moderate.
Airconditioned disco with music to suit all tastes.

BALOOS Larnaca–Dhekelia road.
About 9 km north of town centre next to Vergi Hotel. ● Moderate.
A cocktail bar which also serves snacks.

HORSESHOE Larnaca–Dhekelia road.
8 km north of town centre opposite Palm Beach Hotel. ● Moderate.
A range of exotic cocktails as well as less exotic drinks and snacks.

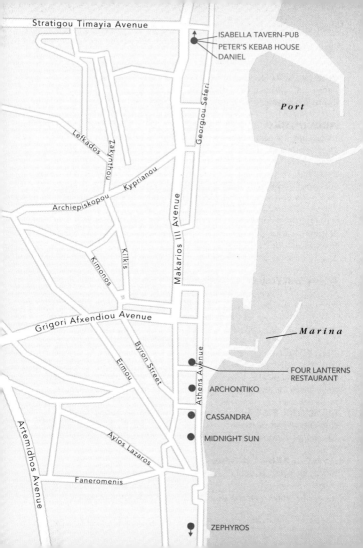

Stratigou Timayia Avenue

ISABELLA TAVERN-PUB
PETER'S KEBAB HOUSE
DANIEL

Port

Georgiou Seferi

Lefkados

Zakynthou

Kyprianou

Archiepiskopou

Makarios III Avenue

Kilkis

Kimonos

Grigori Afxendiou Avenue

Marina

Byron Street

Ermou

Athens Avenue

FOUR LANTERNS
RESTAURANT

ARCHONTIKO

CASSANDRA

MIDNIGHT SUN

Ayios Lazaros

Artemidhos Avenue

Faneromenis

ZEPHYROS

Restaurants

CASSANDRA 101 Athens Avenue. Opposite promenade (Finikoudes). ■ Lunch and dinner. ● Moderate-expensive.
Grills, good Cyprus specialities, pleasant atmosphere and service.

ARCHONTIKO 71 Athens Avenue. Opposite promenade (Finikoudes). ■ Lunch and dinner. ● Moderate-expensive.
In picturesque old building with garden; also open-air on promenade. Grills, Cyprus specialities, fish and international dishes.

ISABELLA TAVERN-PUB Larnaca–Dhekelia road. 9 km from town centre opposite Golden Bay Hotel. ■ All day. ● Moderate.
Snacks, grills and some Cyprus dishes.

DANIEL Larnaca–Dhekelia road. 9 km from town centre opposite Sandy Beach Hotel. ■ All day. ● Moderate.
Snacks, burgers, grills and steaks.

FOUR LANTERNS RESTAURANT Athens Avenue.
■ Lunch and dinner; also cafeteria all day. ● Moderate.
Hotel restaurant with open-air terrace on promenade (Finikoudes). Restaurant serves Cyprus and international cuisine while snacks (including breakfast) and drinks can be obtained in the adjacent cafeteria.

ZEPHYROS 37 Piyale Pasha.
■ Lunch and dinner. ● Moderate.
Fresh fish and good grilled meat. Very popular with Cypriot families out for a day by the sea. Often crowded so the service sometimes suffers.

MIDNIGHT SUN Athens Avenue. Opposite promenade (Finikoudes).
■ All day. ● Inexpensive.
Fast food, hot dog and chips, omelettes, scampi and chips, etc.

PETER'S KEBAB HOUSE Larnaca–Dhekelia road. 7 km from town centre just off main road on land side. ■ Lunch and dinner.
● Inexpensive.
Souvlákia/sheftaliá in pitta bread, grills, snacks; no frills but good value.

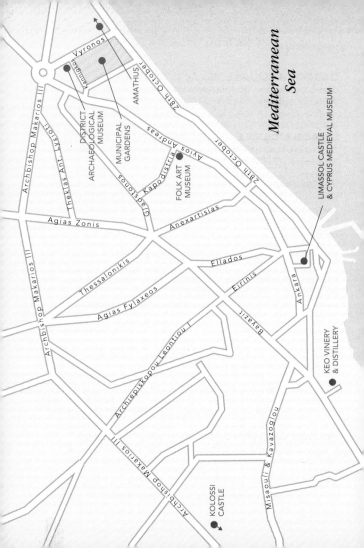

Mediterranean Sea

Vyronos

Kanningos

DISTRICT ARCHAEOLOGICAL MUSEUM

AMATHUS

28th October

MUNICIPAL GARDENS

G. Gregoriou

Kapodistria

Ayios Andreas

28th October

FOLK ART MUSEUM

Archbishop Makarios III

Theklas Ant. Lysioti

Agias Zonis

Anexartisias

LIMASSOL CASTLE & CYPRUS MEDIEVAL MUSEUM

Thessalonikis

Ellados

Eirinis

Ankara

Archbishop Makarios III

Agias Fylaxeos

Bayazit

KEO VINERY & DISTILLERY

Archiepiskopou Leontiou I

Archbishop Makarios III

Misaouli & Kavazoglou

KOLOSSI CASTLE

Attractions

DISTRICT ARCHAEOLOGICAL MUSEUM Kannigkos–Vyronos corner. ■ Summer: 0730-1800 Mon.-Sat., 1000-1300 Sun.; Winter: 0730-1700 Mon.-Sat., 1000-1300 Sun. ● £C0.50.
Artefacts from the Neolithic to Roman periods found near Limassol.

LIMASSOL CASTLE & CYPRUS MEDIEVAL MUSEUM
Near Old Port. ■ Summer: 0730-1800 Mon.-Sat.; Winter: 0730-1800 Mon.-Sat. ● £C0.50.
According to tradition the site where Richard I of England (Richard the Lionheart) married Princess Berengaria of Navarre and crowned her Queen of England. The present building was constructed in the early 14thC on the remains of an earlier Byzantine castle, parts of which are incorporated in it. The medieval collection within the castle contains ceramics and sculpture from the Lusignan and Venetian periods.

FOLK ART MUSEUM 253 Ayios Andreas Street.
▨ Summer: 0830-1300, 1600-1800 Mon., Wed. & Fri., 0830-1300 Tue., Thu. & Sat.; Winter: 0800-1300, 1500-1700 Mon., Wed. & Fri., 0800-1300 Tue., Thu. & Sat. ● £C0.30.
Collection of traditional costumes, and exhibits illustrating folk crafts.

KEO VINERY & DISTILLERY Off Franklin D. Roosevelt Avenue, west of city centre. ■ During working hours. ● Free.
KEO (Kypriakí Etería Oínon) is one of the major producers of wines, beers and spirits on Cyprus. See **LIMASSOL-EXCURSION 1**.

MUNICIPAL GARDENS 28th October Street.
Contains an open-air theatre, and a zoo with mouflon, a breed of moun-tain sheep facing extinction, sometimes seen on the Troodos mountains.

KOLOSSI CASTLE 14 km west of Limassol off Paphos road.
▨ Summer: 0730-1930; Winter: 0730-sunset. ● £C0.50.
Well-preserved medieval castle from the Lusignan period. See **A-Z**.

AMATHUS 11 km east off main coast road close to Amathus Hotel.
Site of one of the ancient city kingdoms of Cyprus. See **A-Z**.

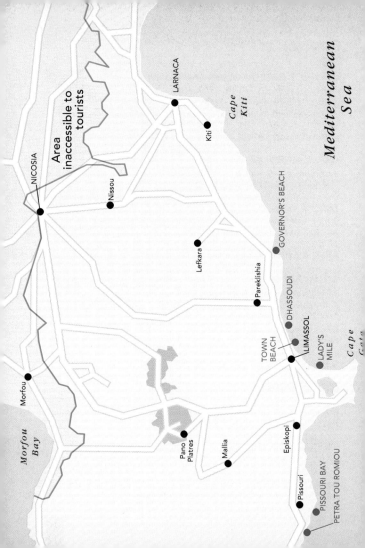

Beaches

The beaches in the central Limassol area are generally not good. To the south of the city lies the port and further north the beaches tend to be narrow and pebbly. The CTO beach at Dhassoudi (see below) is an exception. Many of the seafront hotels have improved their beaches by building breakwaters and importing sand; some of these beaches are available to nonresidents, although a charge may be levied.

GOVERNOR'S BEACH
33 km east of Limassol. Bus in summer, also boat trips.
Part sandy, part rocky. Tavernas. Sometimes overcrowded.

DHASSOUDI
5 km east of Limassol. Bus, also within walking distance of some hotels.
*Run by Cyprus Tourism Organization (see **A-Z**). Extensive sandy beach. Restaurant, beach bar, changing facilities. Good selection of water sports. Shaded areas. Car parking.*

TOWN BEACH
Running along 28th October Street.
Narrow, pebbly and rocky beach, and therefore not very attractive. A number of cafés and kiosks.

LADY'S MILE
5 km west of Limassol. Car.
Extensive sandy beach. Busy at weekends. Cafés. Strong sea currents.

PISSOURI BAY
43 km west of Limassol. Car.
Extensive beach of coarse sand bounded by cliffs. Tavernas and a solitary hotel. Limited range of water sports.

PETRA TOU ROMIOU
49 km west of Limassol. Car.
*Pebbly beach. Superb setting but not very suitable for young children or inexperienced swimmers owing to undertow near rocks. Tourist pavilion on other side of main road. See **LIMASSOL-EXCURSION 1**, **A-Z**.*

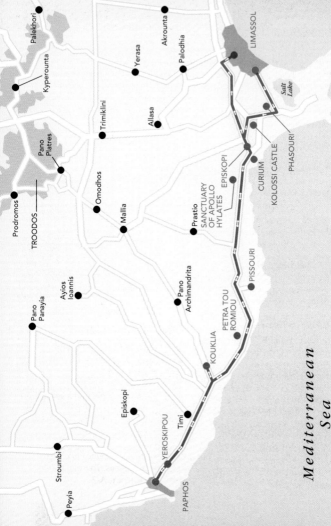

Excursion 1

140 km. A full-day excursion visiting Kolossi Castle, the site of ancient Curium, Petra tou Romiou, the Sanctuary of Aphrodite and Paphos. If all the ancient monuments are to be visited an early start is essential.

Leave Limassol to the southwest past the KEO Vinery (see **LIMASSOL-ATTRACTIONS**) in the direction of Phasouri (avoid the motorway which, although the quickest and most traffic-free route to Paphos, bypasses the earlier stages of this excursion). The area around Phasouri is one of the major citrus-growing regions of Cyprus and the tall windbreaks planted around the plantations form a canopy over the road. Arriving at a T-junction turn right to Kolossi (the left-hand turning leads to the RAF base at Akrotiri – see **A-Z**).

11 km – Kolossi Castle (see **LIMASSOL-ATTRACTIONS, A-Z**). Visit the castle's imposing square keep. Continue along the road until you meet the main road and turn left towards Episkopi. Immediately after climbing a steep escarpment you arrive at the site of ancient Curium on the left.

18 km – Curium (see **A-Z**). Visit the ancient site which contains a number of buildings, notably the spectacularly situated amphitheatre, an early Christian basilica and a number of mosaics. Continue for 1 km along the main road, where a right turn leads to the remains of the stadium of ancient Curium and another right-hand turn a further kilometre along the main road leads to the Sanctuary of Apollo Hylates (see **A-Z**). The main road then goes inland through vine-growing country past the village of Pissouri on the hillside to the left before dramatically sloping down to a sharp right-hand bend to rejoin the coast.

Paphos

49 km – Petra tou Romiou (see LIMASSOL-BEACHES, **A-Z**). The legendary birthplace of Aphrodite (see **A-Z**). A few kilometres further on the road once again tracks inland and some 7 km from Petra tou Romiou a right turn leads to the village of Kouklia, the site of ancient Paphos (see **A-Z**). The site of the Sanctuary of Aphrodite, according to legend dedicated to the goddess by Agapenor, a hero of the Trojan War, can be visited, although it is perhaps of more interest to the archaeologist than the passing visitor. A large farmhouse dating from the Turkish period acts as a museum for artefacts from the site. Returning to the main road, modern Paphos is reached, via Yeroskipou (see **A-Z**), after a further 16 km.

71 km – Paphos (see **A-Z**). The area around modern Paphos contains a number of important archaeological sites. To return to Limassol you will need to retrace your outward route as there is no viable alternative. However, a few kilometres and some busy traffic can be avoided by not taking the turning to Kolossi and staying on the main road which joins the motorway system ringing the city.

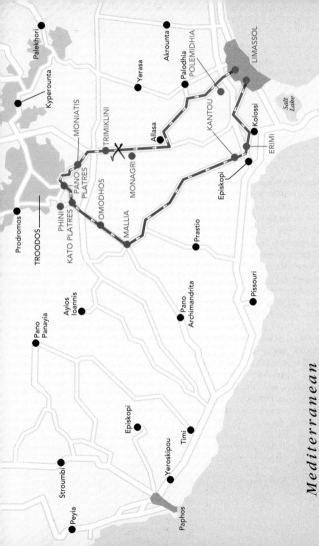

Excursion 2

86 km. A half-day excursion to the attractive countryside around the popular mountain resort of Pano Platres. The roads followed are generally of good condition, although being mountain roads necessarily have some sharp bends. If time permits a walk in the cool forests around Platres is recommended.

Take the road leading west out of Limassol, as if you were travelling to Paphos. Shortly after leaving the urban area, just beyond the village of Erimi, take a right turn. The road passes through the village of Kantou to reach the bed of the river Kouris then climbs steeply to the right.

29 km – Mallia. Take a right turn in the direction of Platres. After travelling through vineyards for some 5 km you will reach Omodhos, a village on the southern slopes of the Troodos mountains (see **A-Z**) with a long tradition of wine making (it has an annual wine festival), in which the monastery of Stavros is situated. The present building dates from the beginning of this century although some of the icons it houses are much earlier. Continuing along the road for a further 6 km you will reach Kato Platres. There are a number of small potteries in this area and also at Phini, 2 km to the north. Continue through Kato Platres to reach the mountain resort of Pano Platres.

44 km – Pano Platres (see **LARNACA-EXCURSION 1**). One of the most popular of the Cyprus mountain resorts (it is 1130 m above sea level), Pano Platres is much loved by walkers. If time permits, the relatively short walk (about 5 km) to the Caledonian falls is worth making. From Pano Platres return to Limassol on the main road past Moniatis.

50 km – Trimiklini. At Trimiklini, with its 18thC church, you will reach a crossroads, one turning of which heads north to Kakopetria and then on to Nicosia. However, take the Limassol turning which, after 5 km, passes to the east of the village of Monagri. A short detour can be made here to visit the monastery of Panayia Amasgou which holds a number of paintings, some dating back to the 12thC. The road continues to Limassol past the former British army camp of Polemidhia, joining the motorway system 2 km from the city centre.

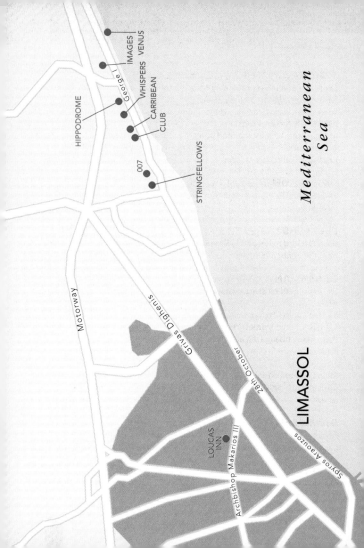

IMAGES

VENUS

George I

WHISPERS

HIPPODROME

CARRIBEAN

CLUB

007

STRINGFELLOWS

Mediterranean
Sea

Motorway

Grivas Dighenis

28th October

LOUCAS
INN

Archbishop Makarios III

Spyros Araouzos

LIMASSOL

VENUS George I Street, Yermasoyia.
On main Yermasoyia road about 6 km from town centre. ● Moderate.
Disco lying adjacent to the beach.

IMAGES Ambelakion corner, George I Street, Yermasoyia.
Just off main Yermasoyia road about 5 km from town centre.
● Moderate.
Cocktails, dancing and videos.

HIPPODROME George I Street, Yermasoyia.
About 5 km from town centre. ● Moderate.
Dancing.

WHISPERS George I Street, Yermasoyia.
On landward side about 5 km from town centre. ● Moderate.
Disco with laser light show.

CARRIBEAN George I Street, Yermasoyia.
On main road close to Yermasoyia hotels. ● Moderate.
Disco.

CLUB George I Street, Yermasoyia.
Next to Carribean (see above). ● Moderate.
Disco.

007 George I Street, Yermasoyia.
On landward side about 4 km from town centre. ● Moderate.
Disco.

STRINGFELLOWS 93a George I Street, Yermasoyia.
About 5 km east, not far from Dhassoudi Beach. ● Moderate.
Cocktail bar with music, billiards, snacks and breakfasts; open 24 hr.

LOUCAS INN 79 Archbishop Makarios III Avenue.
On Limassol bypass about 0.5 km from seafront. ● Inexpensive.
Snacks, drinks and cocktails. Billiards and darts.

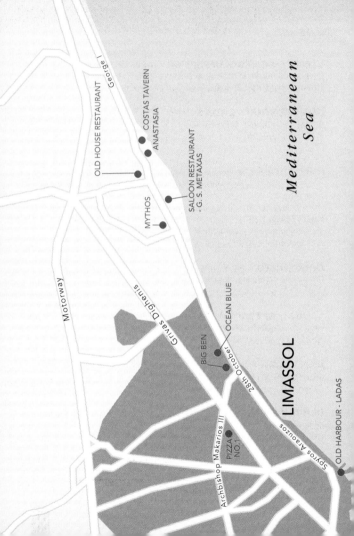

George I

COSTAS TAVERN

ANASTASIA

OLD HOUSE RESTAURANT

SALOON RESTAURANT
- G. S. METAXAS

MYTHOS

Mediterranean
Sea

Motorway

Grivas Dighenis

OCEAN BLUE

BIG BEN

28th October

LIMASSOL

Archbishop Makarios III

PIZZA
NO.1

Spyros Araouzos

OLD HARBOUR - LADAS

Restaurants

OLD HOUSE RESTAURANT Yermasoyia. On main road at Yermasoyia bridge. ▣ Dinner. ● Expensive.
Fish restaurant. Cyprus dancing on certain evenings.

OLD HARBOUR – LADAS Limassol Old Harbour.
▣ Lunch and dinner. ● Expensive.
Wide choice of fish; select from the chilled cabinet. Meat also available.

MYTHOS 47 George I Street, Yermasoyia. Opposite Park Beach Hotel. ▣ Dinner. ● Moderate-expensive.
Cyprus meze and some Cyprus dishes; folk dancing on certain nights.

PIZZA NO. 1 Archbishop Makarios III Avenue. On bypass not far from District Archaeological Museum and Municipal Gardens.
▣ Lunch and dinner. ● Moderate.
Pizzas, grills, salads and sandwiches.

OCEAN BLUE Kanika Complex, 28th October Street. Opposite seafront. ▣ Lunch and dinner. ● Moderate.
Grills, Cyprus specialities and international cuisine.

SALOON RESTAURANT – G. S. METAXAS Dhassoudi. Near Dhassoudi beach entrance. ▣ Lunch and dinner. ● Moderate.
Restaurant and café; everything from snacks to international cuisine.

ANASTASIA Yermasoyia. Off main road just to south of Apollonia Beach Hotel. ▣ Dinner. ● Moderate.
Grills and Cyprus specialities; also Cyprus dancing.

COSTAS TAVERN Yermasoyia. On main road beside Apollonia Beach Hotel. ▣ Dinner. ● Moderate.
Grills and Cyprus specialities.

BIG BEN 327 28th October Street. Opposite seafront.
▣ All day. ● Inexpensive.
Fast food such as burgers, chicken, steaks and ice cream.

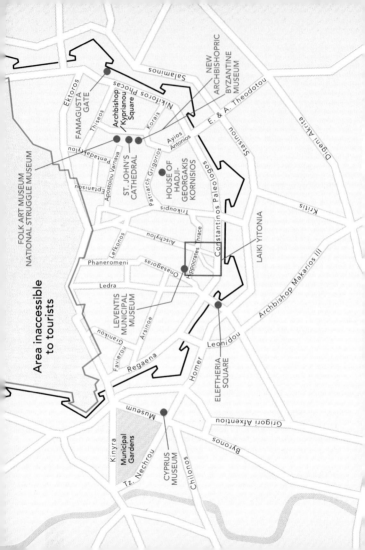

CYPRUS MUSEUM Museum Street. Just outside city walls opposite Municipal Theatre and Gardens. ■ Summer: 0730-1330, 1600-1800 Mon.-Sat., 1000-1300 Sun.; Winter: 0900-1700 Mon.-Sat., 1000-1300 Sun. ● £C1.
The most important archaeological collection on Cyprus, covering all aspects of Cyprus archaeology from the Neolithic age to the Roman era. The Municipal Gardens opposite are a pleasant spot to take a break on a packed tour of the city.

FAMAGUSTA GATE Nikiforos Phocas Avenue.
■ 1000-1300, 1600-1900 Mon.-Fri., 1000-1300 Sat. ● Free.
Once a principal entrance to the walled city, the Famagusta Gate gives a good impression of the massive Venetian fortifications of the city, which nevertheless were unable to withstand the assault of the Ottoman Turks in 1570. It is now the Municipal Cultural Centre and houses exhibitions.

NEW ARCHBISHOPRIC Archbishop Kyprianou Square.
■ Closed to the public.
Built in Venetian style in 1956, its aesthetics are the subject of much public debate.

BYZANTINE MUSEUM Archbishop Kyprianou Square. In New Archbishopric within city walls. ■ Summer: 0930-1300, 1400-1730 Mon.-Fri., 0900-1300 Sat.; Winter: 0900-1300, 1400-1700 Mon.-Fri., 0900-1300 Sat. ● £C0.50.
Holds a fine collection of some 150 icons brought here for safety from churches all over the island. The upper floors house an art gallery.

ST. JOHN'S CATHEDRAL Archbishop Kyprianou Square.
The Orthodox cathedral of Nicosia and seat of the archbishop of Cyprus. It was rebuilt in the 17thC on the site of a former Benedictine monastery. Most of the present murals date from the 18thC.

LAIKI YITONIA
*Pedestrian area just to the northeast of Eleftheria Square (see **NICOSIA-ATTRACTIONS 2**) with a number of carefully restored traditional buildings.*

NICOSIA

FOLK ART MUSEUM

Archbishop Kyprianou Square. In Old Archbishopric within city walls.
▦ 0830-1300, 1400-1600 Mon.-Fri., 0830-1300 Sat. ● £C0.50.
*A collection of costumes, embroidery, and agricultural and domestic
implements, as well as musical instruments, illustrating the history of
everyday life on Cyprus.*

NATIONAL STRUGGLE MUSEUM

Archbishop Kyprianou Square.
▦ June-Aug.: 0730-1330, 1500-1700 Mon.-Fri., 0730-1330 Sat.; Sep.-
May: 0730-1400, 1500-1700 Mon.-Fri., 0730-1300 Sat. ● £C0.25.
*Arms used by the EOKA movement (see **A-Z**) against the British in the
1950s. Also a display of photographs.*

LEVENTIS MUNICIPAL MUSEUM

Hippocrates Street. In Laiki Yitonia.
▦ 1000-1630 Tue.-Sun. ● Free.
*Displays of artefacts illustrating the history of Nicosia from medieval to
modern times.*

Liberty Monument

Laiki Yitonia

HOUSE OF HADJIGEORGAKIS KORNISIOS

Patriarch Grigorios Street. Within city walls near Archbishopric.

▦ Summer: 0730-1330 Mon.-Sat.; Winter: 0730-1400 Mon.-Fri., 0730-1300 Sat. ● £C0.50.

Once the house of Hadjigeorgakis Kornisios, Great Dragoman of Cyprus (guide-interpreter) from 1779 to 1809, this is an excellent example of 18thC domestic architecture, and is now home to an ethnographic collection.

ELEFTHERIA SQUARE

Just south of the main modern access to the walled city, Eleftheria Square is at the centre of modern Nicosia. Running to the north within the walls is Ledra Street, once the main shopping street, and running east off the south of the square is Archbishop Makarios III Avenue where many up-market shops are now situated.

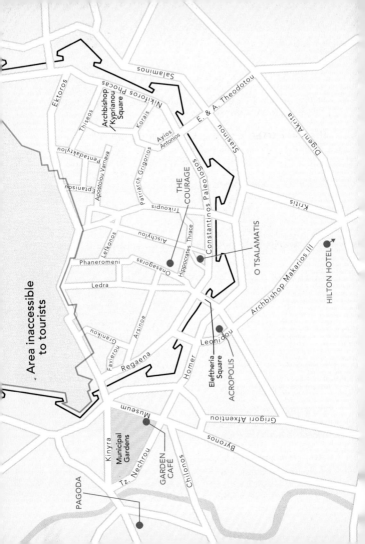

Area inaccessible to tourists

Ektoros

Thiseos

Salaminos

Nikiforos Phocas

Archbishop / Kyprianou Square

E. & A. Theodotou

Korais

Pentadaktilou

Apostolou Varnava

Eptanisou

Patriarch Grigorios

Ayios Antonios

Stasinou

Digeni Akrita

Trikoupis

THE COURAGE

Constantinos Paleologos

Kritis

Aischylou

Leftkonos

Onasagoras

Phaneromeni

Hippocrates

Thrace

O TSALAMATIS

Ledra

Archbishop Makarios III

HILTON HOTEL

Granikou

Arsinoe

Favierou

Leonidou

Regaena

Homer

Eleftheria Square

ACROPOLIS

Kinyra

Municipal Gardens

Museum

Tz. Nechrou

GARDEN CAFÉ

Chilonos

Grigori Afxentiou

Byronos

PAGODA

Restaurants

Unlike the coastal resorts where the visitor is spoilt for choice, central Nicosia does not have a wide range of taverna-style restaurants. If you're in the city centre (Eleftheria Square) a good bet is to head for Laiki Yitonia (see **NICOSIA-ATTRACTIONS 1**).

HILTON HOTEL Archbishop Makarios III Avenue.
■ Lunch and dinner. ● Expensive.
The coffee shop (airconditioned) and pool-side snack bar make a refreshing escape from the midday heat. International cuisine is served but there are some Cyprus dishes too. In addition, the hotel has a more formal restaurant (also airconditioned)

PAGODA 11 Loukis Akritas Street.
■ Lunch and dinner. ● Expensive.
One of the first Chinese restaurants to be opened on Cyprus, and still popular after 20 years.

O TSALAMATIS Centrally situated in Laiki Yitonia.
■ Lunch and dinner. ● Moderate.
Traditional Çyprus food. Good value.

ACROPOLIS 14-16 Leonidou Street.
■ Lunch and dinner. ● Moderate.
Mainly Cyprus cooking but there are also some international dishes. A good place to find some of the less common Cyprus specialities (sheep's head, suckling pig – according to availability). The restaurant has an informal atmosphere and caters for a mainly Cypriot clientele.

GARDEN CAFÉ Municipal Gardens. Opposite Cyprus Museum.
■ Lunch and dinner. ● Inexpensive.
Snacks (burgers, toasted sandwiches) and drinks.

THE COURAGE 9 Pasicratous Street. In street running parallel to Onasagoras Street near main shopping area.
■ Lunch. ● Inexpensive.
For a quick lunch while shopping – very Cypriot!

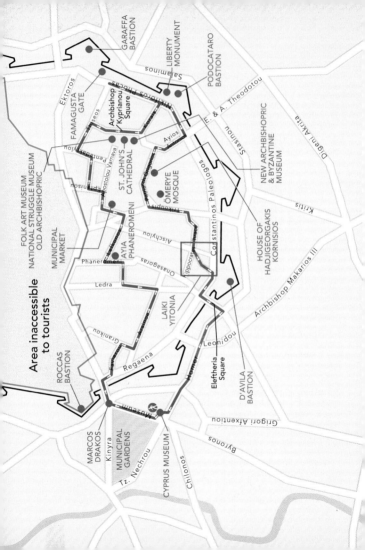

The old walled city of Nicosia is best explored on foot; its narrow streets, one-way systems and pedestrian areas make it a nightmare for drivers. Since pavements are narrow or entirely absent you will need to be alert for traffic. Temperatures in summer can be very high and the early morning or late afternoon are more suitable for this walk; you should also check the opening hours of any museums you may wish to visit (see **NICOSIA-ATTRACTIONS 1 & 2**).

Duration: 1.5-2 hr.
Start outside the Cyprus Museum and follow Museum Street north past the Municipal Theatre and Gardens on your left. At the roundabout with a statue of the EOKA (see **A-Z**) hero Marcos Drakos at its centre, take the third exit to enter the walled city through the Paphos Gate. The fortifications (Roccas Bastion) on your left are one of the 11 bastions forming part of the city walls, over 3 km in circumference and built by the Venetians in the 16thC. At this point you are right on the Green Line (see **A-Z**) and should be careful to obey the restrictions on photography. Once inside the walls turn right into Regaena Street and then left into Favierou Street, turning right then left into Arsinoe Street. Follow this typical Nicosia street until it intersects with Ledra Street, where you should turn left. Ledra Street was once the main shopping street although many of the more fashionable shops now lie outside the walls in Makarios III Avenue. While walking down Ledra Street look for the right turn into Socrates Street which will take you through to Phaneromeni Street where you should turn left to pass Ayia Phaneromeni, one of the main Nicosia churches (built in 1872 but of no great historic interest), on your right. Before you reach the Green Line a right turn will take you into

New Archbishopric

Lefkonos Street, turning left then right past the Municipal Market and left again into Eptanisou Street. After a short distance turn right to reach Pentadaktylou Street and then right into Thiseos Street. A further right turn will take you into Archbishop Kyprianou Square where you will find St. John's Cathedral and the Archbishopric. The Folk Art Museum is situated in the Old Archbishopric and you can also pause to visit the Byzantine Museum in a wing of the New Archbishopric. The National Struggle Museum is also in the square. Turning left out of Archbishop Kyprianou Square along Korais Street will take you to the city walls and the Liberty monument. A short detour can be made by turning left along Nikiforos Phocas Street to the Famagusta Gate in the Garaffa Bastion. Returning along Nikiforos Phocas Street, just after passing the Podocataro Bastion, turn right into Ayios Antonios Street then left into Patriarch Grigorios Street where you will find the house of the 18thC great dragoman of Cyprus, Hadjigeorgakis Kornisios. Continuing along Tylliria Square you pass the 16thC Ömerye mosque on your left to reach Trikoupis Street, where you should turn left. When this street forks, take the right fork into Thrace Street then Hippocrates Street, where you will find the restored area of Laiki Yitonia on your left. Passing through Laiki Yitonia, turn right into Constantinos Paleologos Street which, after passing the D'Avila Bastion (which contains the town hall and post office) on your left, will bring you to Eleftheria Square. Turn left across the moat (now a public garden) and take a right turn into Homer Avenue which will take you back to your starting point in Museum Street.

PAPHOS

TOMBS OF
THE KINGS

Tafon ton Vasileon

Geo...
rgiou Christoforou

Gladstonos

Martiou 25

Exo

DISTRICT
MUSEUM

BYZANTINE
MUSEUM

ETHNOGRAPHICA
MUSEUM

Adamantiou Korai

Apostolou Pavlou

Ifaistou

Agapinoros

Priamou

Daidalou

Ploutarchou

Apostolou Pavlou

KATO
PAPHOS

Ikarou

PAPHOS
MOSAICS

SARANDA
KOLONES

Kyriakou Nikolaou

Paras Afroditis

Stasandrou

Ayios
Antonios

Apollonos

Iasonos

Apostolou Pavlou

Poseidonos

Poseidonos

PAPHOS FORT

AYIA
CHRYSOPOLITISSA
CHURCH

Attractions

DISTRICT MUSEUM Leoforos Georgiou Griva Digheni.
▩ Summer: 0730-1330, 1600-1800 Mon.-Sat., 1000-1300 Sun.;
Winter: 0730-1400, 1500-1700 Mon.-Fri., 0730-1300, 1500-1700 Sat.,
1000-1300 Sun. ● £C0.50.
15thC BC-6thC AD archaeological artefacts found in the Paphos district.

BYZANTINE MUSEUM Martiou 25 Street.
▩ Summer: 0900-1300, 1600-1900 Mon.-Fri., 0900-1300 Sat.;
Winter: 0900-1300, 1500-1700 Mon.-Fri., 0900-1300 Sat. ● £C0.25.
Collection of icons and religious paintings from the 15th-18thC.

ETHNOGRAPHICAL MUSEUM 1 Exo Vrisy Street.
▩ Summer: 0900-1300, 1600-1900 Mon.-Fri., 0900-1300 Sat.;
Winter: 0900-1300, 1500-1700 Mon.-Fri., 0900-1300 Sat. ● £C0.25.
Small collection of items dating from Neolithic age to 19thC farm tools.

TOMBS OF THE KINGS 1 km north of Kato Paphos off coast road
to Coral Bay. ▩ Summer: 0730-1930; Winter: 0730-sunset. ● £C0.50.
Impressive rock-cut tombs dating from 3rdC BC to 3rdC AD.

PAPHOS MOSAICS Kato Paphos.
▩ Summer: 0730-1930; Winter: 0730-sunset. ● £C1.
*Roman mosaics mainly depicting scenes from Greek mythology. The
best known are in the 3rdC AD villas of Theseus and Dionysos.*

SARANDA KOLONES Kato Paphos.
▩ Summer: 0730-1930; Winter: 0730-sunset. ● £C0.50.
Ruins of what was once a spectacular Frankish Crusader castle.

AYIA CHRYSOPOLITISSA CHURCH Kato Paphos.
*15thC church built over site of an earlier Christian basilica. The apostle
Paul is said to have been lashed at a pillar to be seen in the grounds.*

PAPHOS FORT Kato Paphos. ▩ Summer: 0730-1330 Mon.-Sat.;
Winter: 0730-1400 Mon.-Fri., 0730-1300 Sat. ● £C0.50.
Medieval castle, destroyed by Venetians, rebuilt by Turks. Good views.

Cape Arnaouti

A k a m a s

Lachi

Polis

Neo Chorio

Drousia

LARA

Cape Drepanum

Kathikas

Stroumbi

AYIOS GEORGIOS

Peyia

CORAL BAY

CYNTHIANA

Mesoyi

Mediterranean Sea

PAPHOS

Kato Paphos

Yeroskipou

Akhelia

AIRPORT

PAPHOS MUNICIPAL BEACH

YEROSKIPOU PUBLIC BEACH

Beaches

AIRPORT
14 km east of Kato Paphos. Car.
A number of rocky bays in the vicinity of the airport approach road. Wooded picnic areas.

YEROSKIPOU PUBLIC BEACH
4 km southeast of Kato Paphos. Bus.
*Run by Cyprus Tourism Organization (see **A-Z**). Sheltered sandy beach with restaurant, changing facilities, beach bar and a range of water sports. Car parking. See **A-Z**.*

PAPHOS MUNICIPAL BEACH
Kato Paphos. Foot.
Rocky with small man-made sandy sunbathing area. Crowded.

CYNTHIANA
7 km north of Kato Paphos. Car, bus and walk from road (500 m).
Extensive area of rocky bays. Restaurant and hotel. Coral Bay (see below) is a better bet for families with children.

CORAL BAY
10 km north of Kato Paphos. Car, bus.
Extensive sandy beach bounded by cliffs. Rocky at one end. Tavernas, water sports, sun beds. Access may prove difficult for the disabled.

AYIOS GEORGIOS
20 km north of Kato Paphos. Car.
Small fishing shelter with sandy beach. Picturesque setting. Restaurant.

LARA
27 km north of Paphos. Car (preferably four-wheel drive). Also boat trips from Paphos.
Area of deserted, mainly sandy, beaches. This is a nature conservation area within the Akamas National Park and the beach is the nesting ground of loggerhead turtles; there are some restrictions on the use of the beach which are signposted locally.

Excursion

108 km. A one-day excursion to Polis with the opportunity to visit the Baths of Aphrodite. Although this excursion takes in the monastery of Ayios Neophytos with its 16thC murals, its interest is principally scenic.

From Paphos take the main road north signposted Polis. The road climbs gently through wine-growing country. Six kilometres out of Paphos take a left turn to the monastery of Ayios Neophytos.

10 km – Ayios Neophytos. Originally founded in the 12thC, the oldest of the present buildings dates from the 15thC. The church contains murals from the 16thC. The site itself offers excellent views over the coast. After viewing the monastery rejoin the main road and continue north through the village of Stroumbi (largely rebuilt after extensive destruction by an earthquake in 1953) which is noted for its wines. The road descends into the Chrysochou valley and thence into the citrus-growing area of Polis.

44 km – Polis (see **A-Z**). A small town of 2000 inhabitants, relatively unscathed by tourist development, on the site of ancient Marion. Take the minor road leading out of Polis to the west through the fishing village of Lachi and then, along the right fork, to the Baths of Aphrodite.

54 km – Baths of Aphrodite (see **A-Z**). No more than a small shady grotto surrounded by ferns but well worth visiting on account of the

Saranda Kolones

attractive coastline. Refreshment can be obtained at the tourist pavilion. The more energetic may care to walk (or drive if you have a four-wheel drive vehicle) the 5 km along the Akamas peninsula (see **A-Z**) to Fontana Amorosa, no more than a muddy pool but the scenery is well worthwhile. (This area is being used for military exercises when a red flag is flown.) On returning to Polis, while it is of course possible to take the same route back to Paphos, a greater variety of scenery can be enjoyed by taking the road leading southwest through Prodromi, then past the village of Drousia and on to the sultana-producing village of Kathikas, where you should turn right to Peyia.

80 km – Peyia. A detour can be made from Peyia to visit Ayios Georgios and Cape Drepanum, with its small fishing shelter and the offshore island of Yeronisos, by taking the right-hand fork signposted Ayios Georgios.

86 km – Ayios Georgios. Although the site of a 6thC basilica, the church by the café is of recent construction. Return on the same track to Peyia and turn right to return to Kato Paphos past the Tombs of the Kings (see **PAPHOS-ATTRACTIONS**) or take a left turn 6 km south of Peyia to reach the town centre.

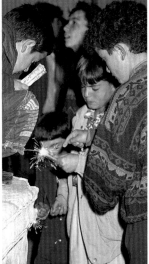

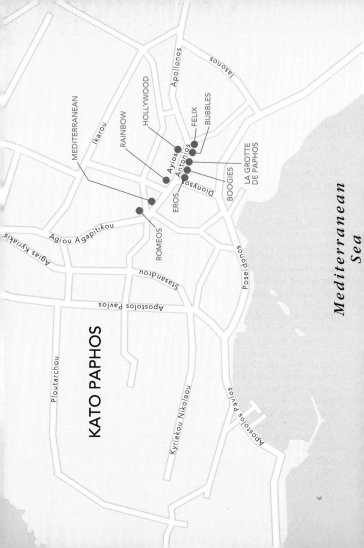

MEDITERRANEAN

Ikarou

RAINBOW

HOLLYWOOD

Apollonos

souosel

FELIX

BUBBLES

Ayios Antonios

LA GROTTE
DE PAPHOS

BOOGIES

EROS

Dionysos

ROMEOS

Agiou Agapitikou

Agias Kyriakis

Stasandrou

Apostolos Pavlos

KATO PAPHOS

Ploutarchou

Poseidonos

Kyriakou Nikolaou

Apostolos Pavlos

*Mediterranean
Sea*

LA GROTTE DE PAPHOS Ayios Antonios Street, Kato Paphos.
On seaward side of street. ● Expensive.
Nightclub with cabaret.

HOLLYWOOD Ayios Antonios Street, Kato Paphos.
On landward side of street. ● Moderate.
Disco in lively entertainment area.

BOOGIES Ayios Antonios Street, Kato Paphos.
On opposite side of street from Hollywood (see above). ● Moderate.
Popular disco-bar.

RAINBOW Ayios Antonios Street, Kato Paphos.
On landward side of street. ● Moderate.
Lively disco.

EROS Ayios Antonios Street, Kato Paphos.
On seaward side of street. ● Moderate.
Well-established and popular disco.

BUBBLES Ayios Antonios Street, Kato Paphos.
On seaward side of street. ● Moderate.
Cocktail bar – very popular gathering point.

FELIX Ayios Antonios Street, Kato Paphos.
Next door to Bubbles (see above). ● Moderate.
Another much-frequented meeting place, especially by the younger set.

MEDITERRANEAN Ayia Napa Street, Kato Paphos.
On continuation of Ayios Antonios Street. ● Moderate.
Lively cocktail bar.

ROMEOS Ayia Napa Street.
In the main nightlife area. ● Inexpensive.
Bar with snooker tables. Serves draught beer.

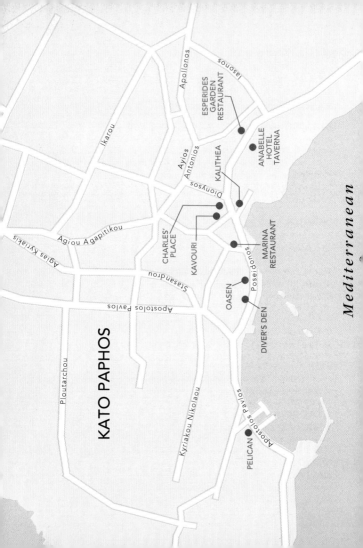

KATO PAPHOS

Mediterranean

Apollonos

Souosei

ESPERIDES
GARDEN
RESTAURANT

ANABELLE
HOTEL
TAVERNA

KALITHEA

Ayios
Antonios

Dionysos

Ikarou

CHARLES'
PLACE

KAVOURI

MARINA
RESTAURANT

Agiou Agapitikou

Agias Kyriakis

Stasandrou

Poseidonos

OASEN

Apostolos Pavlos

DIVER'S DEN

Ploutarchou

Kyriakou Nikolaou

Apostolos Pavlos

PELICAN

Restaurants

ANABELLE HOTEL TAVERNA Poseidonos Street, Kato Paphos.
▦ Lunch and dinner. ● Expensive.
Grills, traditional Cyprus dishes, and good fish and fresh seafood.

CHARLES' PLACE Dionysos Street, Kato Paphos.
▦ Lunch and dinner. ● Moderate.
Grills, fish. Some local specialities including suckling pig and kléftiko.

OASEN Poseidonos Street, Kato Paphos. Opposite seafront.
▦ All day. ● Moderate.
Grills, snacks and ice cream.

MARINA RESTAURANT Alkminis Street, Kato Paphos.
▦ Dinner. ● Moderate.
Cyprus and international cuisine. Live Cyprus music some evenings.

PELICAN Apostolos Pavlos Avenue, Kato Paphos. By old harbour.
▦ Lunch and dinner. ● Moderate.
Specializes in fish and seafood (including expensive lobster!) but meat dishes are also available. One of the oldest restaurants in Paphos.

KAVOURI Artemidos Street, Kato Paphos.
▦ Lunch and dinner. ● Moderate.
Grills, Cyprus dishes. Kléftiko *cooked in traditional oven twice weekly.*

ESPERIDES GARDEN RESTAURANT Poseidonos Street, Kato Paphos. Opposite Anabelle Hotel. ▦ Dinner. ● Moderate.
Grills, and some Cyprus and international cuisine.

DIVER'S DEN Poseidonos Street, Kato Paphos.
▦ Lunch and dinner. ● Inexpensive.
Grills, fish and steaks, and some Cyprus specialities.

KALITHEA Poseidonos Street, Kato Paphos. Near municipal beach overlooking sea. ▦ Lunch and dinner. ● Inexpensive.
Snacks, sandwiches, omelettes – try souvlákia *or* sheftaliá *in pitta bread.*

Tombs of the Kings

Sanctuary of Apollo Hylates

Akamas Peninsula: One of the most isolated parts of Cyprus, the Akamas peninsula lies northwest of Polis. It is an area of rugged low hills which is intended to be designated as a national park, and is of interest to naturalists and walkers. There are marked trails, details of which can be obtained from the Cyprus Tourism Organization (see **A-Z**). See **PAPHOS-EXCURSION**.

Akrites: According to medieval folk poetry, the Akrites were a race of legendary warriors guarding the borders of the Byzantine Empire who achieved outstanding feats of heroism. One of the greatest was Dighenis who, legend tells, jumped from Asia Minor to Cyprus and grasping at the mountains of the northern coast to prevent himself slipping back into the sea, left the imprint of his hand in the rocks. The range is known today as Pentadaktylos, Greek for 'five fingers'.

Akrotiri: Familiar to servicemen as the site of an RAF airfield, the Akrotiri peninsula lies within a Sovereign Base Area (see **A-Z**) but is just as well known among ornithologists as the breeding ground of a number of species of migratory aquatic birds. In the winter months the salt lake is home to large flocks of flamingos. The Akrotiri peninsula is also noted for its citrus plantations. See **LIMASSOL-EXCURSION 1**.

Amathus: 11 km east of Limassol, Amathus is the site of one of the ancient city kingdoms of Cyprus and continuing excavations have revealed a number of tombs. According to legend, Theseus, after his defeat of the Minotaur, brought the pregnant Ariadne to Amathus. See **LIMASSOL-ATTRACTIONS**.

Aphrodite: Aphrodite, the Greek goddess of love, is said to have been born on the southern coast of Cyprus at Petra tou Romiou (see **A-Z**). In antiquity Cyprus was a major centre for the worship of Aphrodite and an extensive temple to her stood at Palea Paphos near the modern village of Kouklia (see **LIMASSOL-EXCURSION 1**).

Apollo Hylates: The god of the woodland was worshipped on Cyprus from the 8thC BC. The Sanctuary of Apollo Hylates is to be

found on the Limassol–Paphos road about 1.5 km west of Curium (see **A-Z**). The buildings you see today, which have been partly reconstructed, mostly date from the 1stC AD. See **LIMASSOL-EXCURSION 1**.

Assinou: See **LARNACA-EXCURSION 1**.

Assinou

Ayia Napa: Pop: 1500. Once a sleepy fishing village built around a monastery dating from the Venetian period, Ayia Napa (meaning 'Holy Forest') has become a major tourist area. One need look no further than the excellent shallow bays with crystal-clear water and sandy beaches to find the reason for its popularity. The monastery with its octagonal marble fountain is still a peaceful spot and worth visiting. The surrounding area has been tastefully landscaped with gardens, and benches to relax upon. See **AYIA NAPA**.

Ayia Napa

Ayios Heracleidos: Lying some 20 km southwest of Nicosia near the site of Tamassos (see **A-Z**), the monastery of Heracleidos, now a nunnery, dates from early times, although the present building was erected in 1759. St. Heracleidos guided saints Paul and Barnabas when they converted Cyprus to Christianity in AD 45 and the church contains a Roman tomb that could be that of the saint himself.

Ayios Ioannis Lampadistis: Originally a monastery, this collection of buildings on the northern slopes of Troodos (see **A-Z**) not far from the village of Kalopanayiotis has a fine collection of murals and well-preserved icons.

Ayios Nikolaos: Also known as St. Nicholas of the Roof, this church is situated near Kakopetria (see **A-Z**) high in the Troodos mountains (see **A-Z**) and is renowned for its frescoes, some of which date back to the 11thC. It is unusual in that it has an upper roof (dating from the 13thC) to protect the lower domed roof.

Baths of Aphrodite: Loutra tis Aphrodhitis. The worship of Aphrodite (see **A-Z**), goddess of love, has been closely associated with Cyprus since the earliest times. Legend has it that she met with her suitors at these springs a few kilometres west of Polis. The Baths of Aphrodite are worth visiting for the magnificent views over the northwest coast of the island. See **PAPHOS-EXCURSION**.

Cedar Valley: While most Cyprus forests are pine, the cedar is also a native of the island and some 50,000 of these ancient trees, some over 800 years old, can be seen in Cedar Valley in the Troodos mountains (see **A-Z**) west of Kykkos monastery (see **A-Z**).

Chrysorroyiatissa: Founded in the 12thC, the monastery of Panayia Chrysorroyiatissa lies in the foothills of the Troodos mountains (see **A-Z**) 40 km east of Paphos, from where it is best reached. It can also be reached from Kykkos monastery (see **A-Z**) along a forest road. The present buildings date from 1770. As well as holding an important collection of icons, the monastery produces high-quality wines!

Curium: The ancient city kingdom of Curium (or Kourion), 19 km west of Limassol and one of the most important and interesting archaeological sites on Cyprus, is thought to date from the colonization of the island by Mycenaean Greeks in the 14thC BC, although the buildings visible today are from a much later period. The amphitheatre with its magnificent backdrop of Akrotiri Bay, dating from the 2ndC BC and enlarged in the 2ndC AD, is still used for plays and concerts. Buildings from the 5thC AD include remains of the massive basilica and the house of Eustolios with its mosaic floors. The partly reconstructed stadium lies on the other side of the main Limassol–Paphos road. There is a restaurant operated by the Cyprus Tourism Organization (see **A-Z**) on the main Curium site. See **LIMASSOL-EXCURSION 1**.

EOKA: Ethnikí Orgánosi Kypríon Agonistón (National Organization for the Cypriot Struggle) was the name of the terrorist organization formed in 1955 to fight the British colonial government. Often referred to as an independence movement, its aim was in fact the union of Cyprus with Greece. Memorials to EOKA fighters are to be seen all over Cyprus. A second EOKA movement, EOKA B, emerged in the early 1970s to challenge the government of the republic which it believed had betrayed the ideal of union, events that ultimately led to the Turkish invasion of 1974. The British visitor has no need to worry since any hard feelings of the EOKA days have long been forgotten by the Cypriots who, despite past events, hold the British in much affection. A very personal account of the emergence of the EOKA movement is given in the book *Bitter Lemons* by Lawrence Durrell, who was living on Cyprus at the time. See **NICOSIA-ATTRACTIONS 2**.

Episkopi: A village 10 km west of Limassol that has given its name to the extensive Sovereign Base Area (see **A-Z**) that is the Near East headquarters for the Royal Air Force. The Limassol–Paphos road runs through the base (there is a public right of way) and as you drive through it, a distance of some 8 km, you will notice the serried rows of office buildings and married quarters as well as the sports ground forming a piece of Britain incongruously placed in the middle of the Cyprus landscape.

Fig Tree Bay: A small sandy bay with a limited although increasing amount of tourist development about 10 km south of the Turkish-occupied zone at the eastern end of the island. See AYIA NAPA-BEACHES, EXCURSION.

Folk Dancing: This will probably only be seen at one of the Cyprus evenings held in some restaurants and hotels.

Galata: A village in the Troodos mountains (see **A-Z**) noted for its painted churches (Ayios Sozomenos, Panayia Theotokos, Panayia Eleousa and Ayia Paraskevi) in or around it dating from the 16thC. The churches of Panayia Eleousa and Panayia Theotokos comprise the extant buildings of the monastery of Podithou. See LARNACA-EXCURSION 1.

Green Line: The name given to the border of the Turkish-occupied zone.

Grivas (1898-1974): A Cypriot colonel in the mainland Greek army, later made a general, who under the code name Dighenís was the leader of the underground EOKA (see **A-Z**) terrorist movement that fought against the British in the 1950s. Appointed Minister of Defence after independence he was later exiled to Greece, only to return later clandestinely to form the EOKA B movement that ultimately resulted in the coup d'état of 1974, although he died some months before the fateful events that led to the Turkish invasion.

Hala Sultan Tekke: See LARNACA-ATTRACTIONS 2, EXCURSION 2.

Kakopetria: One of the most picturesque of the Troodos (see **A-Z**) villages, Kakopetria is a favourite refuge for the Cypriots from the summer heat. It is also noted for its cherry crop. See **LARNACA-EXCURSION 1**.

Khirokitia: The best-preserved of the Neolithic settlements on the island, Khirokitia lies west of the Nicosia–Limassol motorway 48 km south of Nicosia (leave the motorway at Junction 14). The main street of the settlement, dating from 6800 BC, is visible and surrounded by amazingly cramped beehive-shaped houses which are tightly clustered on the hillside. A number of artefacts excavated from the site are on display at the Cyprus Museum (see **NICOSIA-ATTRACTIONS 1**). See **LAR-NACA-EXCURSION 1**.

Kiti: See **LARNACA-EXCURSION 2**.

Kolossi Castle: Built in the 13thC and reconstructed in the 15thC, the castle served as the headquarters of the Knights of St. John of Jerusalem who administered large estates producing sugar cane and the sweet red wine known as Commandaria (see **Drinks**). For those prepared to brave the narrow winding staircase the battlements offer good views over the surrounding countryside. See **LIMASSOL-ATTRACTIONS, EXCURSION 1**.

Kykkos: The richest and largest monastery in Cyprus, Kykkos, founded in 1100, is a popular place of pilgrimage. It occupies an isolated position on the northwest slopes of Troodos (see **A-Z**). Dedicated to the Virgin Mary, it contains an icon of the Virgin given by the Byzantine emperor Alexis Comnenos and said to be painted by St. Luke the Evangelist himself. Archbishop Makarios III, first President of Cyprus (see **Makarios**), was a novice in the monastery and is buried at Throni about 3 km away.

Larnaca: Pop: 53,000. Larnaca can claim to be the oldest inhabited city in Cyprus. Legend has it that it was founded by Noah's grandson, Kittim, who gave it its ancient name of Kition. Archaeological evidence indicates that it was occupied by Mycenaean Greeks in the 14th or 13thC BC, although it was later conquered by Phoenicians whose rule lasted until the 4thC BC. The philosopher Zeno was born in Larnaca in 336 BC. Lazarus, after being raised from the dead by Christ, became the town's first bishop and the present-day church of Ayios Lazaros was erected by the emperor Leo VI in the 9thC on the site of his tomb. The importance of the town diminished and was not regained until the days of Ottoman rule when it became an important commercial centre and the island's principal port. Nowadays Limassol has eclipsed its importance as a port (although there is still a small container port north of the town) but Larnaca boasts an attractive marina as well as Cyprus' main airport. A number of hotels lie to the northeast of the town beyond the oil refinery and oil installations. See **LARNACA**.

Lefkara: The village of Lefkara, or rather the two villages of Kato (lower) and Pano (upper) Lefkara, lies 11 km northwest of the junction of the Nicosia–Limassol motorway with the Larnaca road about 50 km from Larnaca. It is the major centre for the traditional form of embroidery known as *lefkarítika*. According to tradition, Leonardo da Vinci, during a visit to Cyprus, chose this needlework of exceptional quality for the altar cloth of Milan cathedral – although it should be added that there is no firm evidence that he ever visited the island! See **LARNACA-EXCURSION 1**, **Crafts**.

Limassol: Pop: 120,000. This is the major port of Cyprus and an important commercial and industrial centre, as well as the headquarters of the Cyprus wine industry. Although there is evidence of settlement as early as the second millennium BC, Limassol did not gain much importance until the time of the Crusades. The key historic site is the castle, where Richard the Lionheart is reputed to have married Princess Berengaria of Navarre. See **LIMASSOL, LARNACA-EXCURSION 1**.

Macheras: Founded in 1148, Macheras monastery occupies a picturesque setting 40 km southwest of Nicosia.

Makarios (1913-77): Archbishop Makarios III, born Michail Mouskos, was the political and religious leader of the Cypriot Greeks during the EOKA (see **A-Z**) period in the 1950s and became the first President of Cyprus on independence in 1960. He escaped the island during the coup d'état in July 1974, returning later to resume his presidency until his death in 1977. He is buried at Throni near Kykkos monastery (see **A-Z**), where he served his novitiate. It may seem curious to the British visitor that a cleric should also hold high political office, but under the Ottoman occupation the Archbishop of Cyprus had always acted as the leader or ethnarch of the Greek community and in this sense Makarios III was only continuing a traditional role.

Monasteries: Cyprus is dotted with numerous monasteries, many of great antiquity. Most of the Cyprus monasteries are sited on high ground away from the reaches of coastal raiders and are important repositories of Byzantine art; many have priceless icons and frescoes. Indeed, Cyprus is of particular importance to the historian of Byzantine art since, being situated on the fringes of the Byzantine Empire, it was spared much of the destructive attentions of the iconoclasts (Greek for 'breakers of images') of the 8th and 9thC.
Most monasteries welcome visitors (although some have certain restrictions on women) but you should remember they are places of prayer and pilgrimage and thus you should dress and behave accordingly.

Myths & Legends: See **Akrites, Aphrodite**.

Nicosia: Pop: 167,000. This is the largest city on Cyprus and the island's capital since the 11thC. Although inhabited from the Bronze Age it only flowered during the Lusignan period with the building of a royal palace and some fifty churches. The massive fortifications that still enclose the old city were built by the Venetians in the 16thC. The Archbishopric of Cyprus lies within the walls close to the 17thC Orthodox cathedral. The Folk Art Museum and Byzantine Museum conveniently lie on the same square. To the southwest of the walls lies the Cyprus Museum, across the road from the Municipal Theatre and Gardens. The main shopping areas are Ledra Street, within the walls, and Archbishop Makarios III Avenue to the south on the other side of Eleftheria Square. See **NICOSIA, LARNACA-EXCURSION 1**.

Northern Cyprus: Following an abortive coup by EOKA B (see **A-Z**) in 1974, the Turkish army invaded Cyprus and still holds the northern part of the island. Subsequently the Turkish Cypriots unilaterally declared the 'Turkish Republic of Northern Cyprus' which occupies 37% of the island's total land area. This 'republic' is not recognized by the international community, the government of the Republic of Cyprus being recognized as the sole de jure government of the entire island. The resulting situation for the visitor is curious. On one hand he or she is in theory just as welcome to visit the occupied parts of Cyprus as he or she is to visit any other part of Cyprus, these being an integral part of the Republic of Cyprus. On the other hand the government of the Republic of Cyprus naturally strongly disapproves of any action which would appear to give recognition to an 'administration' it and the rest of the world regards as illegal or to make use of property that was seized from its rightful owners without compensation during the 1974 invasion. It will be appreciated that to do the former without at the same time doing the latter is well-nigh impossible. In practice, most visitors remain to the south of the Green Line (see **A-Z**). Although discouraged, it is, however, technically possible to cross into the North subject to certain restrictions which may, of course, vary from time to time. Such crossings may only be made at the Ledra Palace Hotel checkpoint in Marcos Drakos Avenue in Nicosia. You may only cross during the daylight hours and must return the same day. You will need your

passport but it is important that you do not have it stamped on the
Turkish side as this could lead to problems when you return (use a
loose sheet of paper for any visas or stamps). Also you will not be
allowed to take a hired car across; you will need to cross on foot and
make fresh travel arrangements on the other side.

You should note that since 1974 there has been a continuing attempt to
'Turkisize' the occupied area and thus much of the practical information in this book will not apply in the North. You should also note that a
number of place names have been changed.

The visitor should also remember that feelings over the events of 1974
run high, especially among those that lost relatives and the nearly
200,000 Greek Cypriots who were made homeless. Tact should be
exercised when discussing the occupied part of Cyprus and it is unreal-
istic to expect the enthusiastic assistance, normally so forthcoming in
Cyprus, when planning a crossing of the Green Line.

Nonetheless there are a number of archaeological and historical sites of
interest in the occupied part:

Bellapais: The 13thC Abbey of Peace (Abbaye de la Paix), now partly
ruined, was founded by the Lusignans and enjoys a remarkable situation overlooking the northern coast.

Buffavento: One of three Lusignan castles (see also Kantara and St.
Hilarion below) situated in the Pentadaktylos mountains. Buffavento
was dismantled by the Venetians and now little more than rubble
remains.

Famagusta: In Lusignan times this was one of the richest cities in the
eastern Mediterranean. Under Venetian rule it became the setting for
Shakespeare's *Othello* but was badly destroyed in a year-long siege
before capitulating to the Turks in 1571. The modern town to the south
of the Venetian fortifications, with its miles of sandy beaches, was
Cyprus' principal tourist resort until the Turkish invasion of 1974. To the
north of Famagusta is the Graeco-Roman city of Salamis (see below).

Kantara: The most easterly of the three Lusignan castles on the
Pentadaktylos range (see also Buffavento and St. Hilarion).

Kyrenia: A picturesque port on the north coast dominated by a massive
castle, originally built by the Byzantines, rebuilt by the Lusignans in
1208, with further fortifications added by the Venetians. The castle

contains a ship wrecked off the Kyrenia coast in 300 BC.

Nicosia (Turkish Quarter): Selemiye mosque, Selemiye Street: An excellent example of Lusignan Gothic architecture. Originally the cathedral of St. Sophia, its construction commenced in 1209, and was converted into a mosque in 1570.

Bedestan: Next to the Selemiye mosque (see above), this was once the church of St. Nicholas and was later used as a textile market.

Büyük Khan: A little to the west of the Selemiye mosque. A caravanserai since the 16thC, it was turned into a prison in the early days of British rule and is now under restoration.

St. Hilarion: A spectacularly-situated Lusignan castle perched on the mountains (730 m) overlooking Kyrenia (see also Buffavento and Kantara).

Salamis: Once the leading city kingdom of Cyprus, complete with amphitheatre, baths and a gymnasium. Artefacts dating from the 11thC BC have been found at Salamis, said to be founded by Teucer, son of the king of the Greek island of Salamis. Rebuilt in the 4thC AD by the Byzantine emperor Constantine II, it was renamed Constantia and became the capital of Cyprus.

Omodhos: See LIMASSOL-EXCURSION 2.

Panayia tou Araka: At Laghoudhera in the Troodos mountains (see A-Z), lying about 1 km off the main road, this church contains some of the finest frescoes on Cyprus dating from the 12thC. You may have to ask locally for the key.

Odeon, Paphos

Paphos: Pop: 23,000. The most westerly town on Cyprus and the site of the country's second airport (13 km from the town centre). The modern part of the town is known as Ktima while Kato Paphos (once confusingly known as Nea Paphos – 'New Paphos') lies about 2 km to the south and contains the picturesque harbour and fort as well as many important archaeological sites. It should be noted that Palea Paphos – 'Old Paphos' – is by the modern village of Kouklia, some 16 km to the southeast, and was an important centre for the worship of Aphrodite (see **A-Z**).

The modern town of Ktima holds little of historic interest, although it does have an archaeological collection at the District Museum as well as a Byzantine Museum.

Among the many sites of archaeological interest in Kato Paphos are the fine 3rdC AD Roman mosaics in the House of Dionysos, the 3rdC BC Tombs of the Kings carved from the surrounding rock, the remains of the Frankish Crusader castle of Saranda Kolones (literally 'forty columns') and the pillar at which St. Paul, who together with St. Barnabas brought Christianity to Cyprus in 45 AD, was lashed. The small fishing harbour, overlooked by the fort (originally erected in the

14thC on the site of an earlier castle, blown up by the Venetians and later partly rebuilt by the Turks in the 16thC) has a number of bars and restaurants on the waterfront. See **PAPHOS**, **LIMASSOL-EXCURSION 1**.

Peristerona: See **LARNACA-EXCURSION 1**.

Petra tou Romiou: These much-photographed limestone rocks by the main Limassol–Paphos road are the legendary birthplace of Aphrodite (see **A-Z**), and one of the most attractive parts of the Cyprus coastline. If you do swim from the adjacent pebbly beach be careful of currents eddying around the rocks. See **LIMASSOL-BEACHES**, **EXCURSION 1**.

Pissouri Bay: See **LIMASSOL-BEACHES**.

Platres: See **LARNACA-EXCURSION 1**, **LIMASSOL-EXCURSION 2**.

Polis: Pop: 2000. A citrus-growing centre and the main town of the northwest of the island which you will probably pass through if you visit the Baths of Aphrodite (see **A-Z**). A city called Marion, said to be founded by the Athenians in the 7thC BC, stood close to the site of modern Polis. Its wealth was founded on copper mining carried out in the surrounding hills, and until the 1970s copper ores were still exported from Karavostasi, 50 km to the east of Polis. See **PAPHOS-EXCURSION**.

Protaras: The resort lies on Cyprus' east coast and has a fine sandy beach which has been developed as a tourist resort since the 1974 invasion. See **AYIA NAPA-BEACHES**, **EXCURSION**.

St. Barnabas: A native of Salamis (see **Northern Cyprus**) who, together with the apostle Paul, brought Christianity to Cyprus, converting the proconsul of Paphos, Sergius Paulus, in 45 AD.

Salt Lakes: The two salt lakes are at Larnaca (near the airport) and at Akrotiri (see **A-Z**) west of Limassol. Both are home to populations of migrant flamingos between Oct. and Mar., as well as many other species of interest to the ornithologist. See **LARNACA-EXCURSION 2**.

Stavrovouni: Situated on an isolated peak (685 m) 17 km west of Larnaca, the monastery of Stavrovouni offers superb views over all the surrounding coast for those brave enough to tackle the road leading to it. The monastery is said to have been founded by St. Helena, mother of Constantine the Great, although the present building dates only to the last century, when it was extensively rebuilt. Women are not allowed to enter the monastery itself. See **LARNACA-EXCURSION 1**.

Tamassos: Lying about 20 km southwest of Nicosia is the site of an ancient city state famed for its copper mines mentioned in Homer's *Odyssey*. Although little remains of the city some tombs have been discovered and excavations are continuing. See **Ayios Heracleidos**.

Trooditissa: One of the more noted Troodos monasteries, 5 km northwest of Platres, it was reputedly founded in the 13thC, although the present building is not of great antiquity, dating from 1731. It is the site of a large fair on 15 Aug.

Troodos: The largest range of mountains on Cyprus. Its highest point is Mount Olympus (1950 m) and the golf ball-like structures on the summit are part of a radar early-warning system. Most of the Troodos range is covered in pine forests dotted with picturesque villages and monasteries, and it is excellent country for keen walkers. See **LARNACA-EXCURSION 1**.

Yeroskipou: A village some 4 km east of Paphos, named after the sacred garden of Aphrodite (see **A-Z**) and noted for *loukoúmi*, a sweet similar to Turkish delight. It is also noted for its five-domed church of Ayia Paraskevi which contains paintings and murals, some dating as far back as the 9thC BC. See **LIMASSOL-EXCURSION 1**, **PAPHOS-BEACHES**.

Accidents & Breakdowns: In the event of an accident exchange names and insurance details. If there is an injury the police should be summoned, tel: 199. If you break down your car hire company should be contacted; alternatively the Cyprus Automobile Association, tel: 02-313233, may be able to help. See **Consulates**, **Driving**, **Emergency Numbers**.

Accommodation: Hotels are graded using a star rating system running from a single star, the lowest category, to five stars, the highest. There are also more modest 'Hotels without a Star'. Hotel apartments are classified as A or B. A double room costs from around £C15 in a one star establishment (less in guesthouses) to £C90 or more in the very best hotels in high season. Beach hotels are often located several kilometres outside towns; you should check the location before booking. It should be remembered that beach hotels are often booked up with block bookings from tour operators and the independent traveller may find it difficult to get rooms during high season. Likewise, hotels in the Troodos mountains are very popular with the Cypriots escaping the heat of the cities. If you do have a problem finding accommodation the Cyprus Tourism Organization (see **A-Z**) may be able to help. Self-catering villas are also available but, unlike Greece, there are only very few rooms in private houses. See **Camping & Caravanning**, **Youth Hostels**.

Airports: The principal airport on Cyprus is at Larnaca, situated on the seafront 6.5 km south of the town. It is served by scheduled services of Cyprus Airways, British Airways and other national carriers as well as charter flights. Although there are some bus services to Larnaca and Limassol (77 km to the west), most travellers prefer to use taxis (see **A-Z**) which are plentiful and good value (approximate cost to Larnaca is £C2, Limassol £C14). Larnaca airport can be very busy in the high season and it is advisable to check-in in good time.
The west of the island is served by Paphos airport, 13 km southeast of the town, and is served by some scheduled services of Cyprus Airways as well as charter operators. Paphos airport is 67 km from Limassol. There is no bus service to Paphos airport; taxis to Paphos town centre cost approximately £C4 and to Limassol £C13.

Antiquities: The export of antiquities (including icons and other works of art) is strictly controlled and export permits from the Department of Antiquities (1 Museum Street, Nicosia) are required. It is also illegal to remove antiquities from archaeological sites or from the sea bed. Public opinion is sensitive on the subject of removal of antiquities and these regulations are liable to be enforced enthusiastically!

Baby-sitters: Many hotels offer a baby-sitting service; it is, however, necessary to make advance arrangements with the reception. See **Children**.

Banks: See **Currency**, **Money**, **Opening Times**.

Beaches: There are excellent beaches all around the Cyprus coastline and generally the water is unpolluted. The sandiest beaches are usually to be found at the eastern end of the island. Many beaches have cafés or restaurants and a variety of water-sports facilities are available at the most popular. Public beaches run by the Cyprus Tourism Organization (see **A-Z**) at Yeroskipou east of Paphos, Dhassoudi east of Limassol and Larnaca Public Beach (10 km east of Larnaca town) have a full range of facilities, including cafés and restaurants, changing rooms and beach furniture. See the **BEACHES** topic pages for **AYIA NAPA**, **LARNACA**, **LIMASSOL** and **PAPHOS**.

Coral Bay

Best Buys: It is said that when Leonardo da Vinci visited Cyprus in the 15thC he was so struck by the local needlework (*lefkarítika*) that he chose it for the altar of Milan cathedral (although there is no evidence that Leonardo actually visited the island). *Lefkarítika*, usually wrongly referred to as lace, is widely available, although not cheap, but beware of imported imitations. Other Cyprus handicrafts such as leatherware, basketwork, copperware and ceramics also make good buys. You can watch these items being made at the Handicraft Centre in Nicosia (see **Crafts**) which has a tempting gift shop. Traditional gold and silver jewellery makes an interesting gift and is usually reasonably priced. Locally-produced clothing and footwear offer good value for money. Curiously, glasses and contact lenses are also good value. See **Markets**.

Bicycle & Motorcycle Hire: Bicycle and motorcycle hire is widely available in all the major towns. While enjoyable in more rural areas, cycling in the centres of the main cities of Limassol and Nicosia is not recommended. Furthermore, cyclists and moped riders should bear in mind that road standards in the mountains can be poor and unsuited to this form of transport. Cyclists and motorcyclists should exercise extreme caution and not expect other road users to make special allowances for them.

Motorcyclists must be over 18, hold a valid national licence and wear crash helmets. Third-party insurance is obligatory and is often the only insurance provided by the basic hire agreement. If you require additional cover, which is advisable, check the documents carefully.

Daily rates are approximately £C2.50 for bicycles and £C4-10 for motorcycles.

Budget: Most items are very reasonably priced on Cyprus but do remember that the Cyprus pound is worth more than the British pound and can give the impression that things are cheaper than they actually are.

Bread (1 kg)	35 cents
Butter (250 g)	25 cents
Eggs (dozen)	42 cents
Fruit Juice (1 litre)	50 cents
Wine (0.75 litre bottle)	60 cents-£C2
Hotel breakfast	approx. £C2
Lunch	approx. £C3
Dinner	approx. £C6
Kebab in pitta bread (takeaway)	approx. £C1.25
Museum ticket	50 cents-£C1

Buses: A number of companies operate bus services within towns as well as between towns and villages. The latter, however, are often unreliable, slow and may employ ancient vehicles. The visitor would be well advised to use the modestly-priced service taxis (see **A-Z**) for travel between towns.

Cameras & Photography: Photographic materials are readily available in all Cyprus towns, as are developing services (including same-day processing). Prices are similar to those in the UK. The photographer should bear in mind that the hot and often humid climate is not kind to film, although this should not cause problems if sensible precautions are taken (do not leave cameras exposed to the sun in cars, etc.). Photography is forbidden near military camps or installations and in particular near the border with the Turkish-occupied zone. A permit is required to take photographs in museums and flash should not be used in churches with murals or icons.

Camping & Caravanning: Camping is restricted to the six official-ly approved camp sites, five on beaches near Limassol, Larnaca, Paphos, Polis and Ayia Napa, and one in the Troodos mountains a few kilometres from Platres. Fees are about £C1.50 for a tent or caravan plus £C1 per person. Camp sites have showers, toilets and washing facilities, and an electricity supply can usually be provided at addition-al cost. Caravans are uncommon in Cyprus.

Car Hire: Car hire is popular among visitors to Cyprus. The major international car hire companies are represented in Cyprus together with a number of local firms. A national or international driving licence is required.

Officially-approved hire cars have a distinctive red numberplate. Rates are from £C13 a day, depending on the size of vehicle. Many firms will not hire cars to persons under 21. Do check the insurance cover being offered; it may be worthwhile considering paying an additional colli-sion damage waiver premium since minor bumps and scratches are not uncommon in Cyprus. Main roads are generally of an acceptable stan-dard but the minor mountain roads can require considerable skill and care. If you are intent on exploring the more remote parts of the island it may be worth considering the hire of a four-wheel drive vehicle. See **Driving**.

Ceremonies: Traditional village weddings are held increasingly rarely these days but if you do have a chance to attend such a ceremo-ny it is well worth taking. A number of tour operators lay on 'weddings' for tourists and these offer an opportunity to get some idea of the music and dancing that traditionally took place.

Chemists: Chemists, which exhibit a sign comprising a green cross with a serpent entwined around it, will be found in all Cyprus towns and stock most items available in the UK. There is a duty chemist rota to ensure that at least one shop in each town remains open after normal hours; details can be found on the doors of most chemists and in the local press, including the English-language *Cyprus Mail*. Regulations regarding the dispensing of some prescription medicines are often interpreted more liberally and if you have the misfortune to have a prescription run out it may be worth speaking to a chemist before resorting to a doctor for a new prescription. See **Health**.

Children: The Cypriots love children and spoil them unashamedly. Restrictions on children entering restaurants and bars are rare. See **Baby-sitters**.

Churches: Most churches on Cyprus are Greek Orthodox. While the visitor is welcome to visit them common sense should be exercised as to dress and behaviour. Some village churches are kept locked unless a service is being held

but the key can usually be obtained – try asking at the nearest café. Larger churches in towns are usually open during daylight hours most days but precise opening hours depend on the priest in charge. If you are travelling any distance with a view to visiting a specific church, it is worthwhile enquiring at the Cyprus Tourism Organization (see **A-Z**) office in your resort as to current practices regarding opening. Admission to churches is free but a donation is always appreciated, and indeed expected if the church has been opened specially for the visitor.

Ayios Lazaros, Larnaca

Climate: Cyprus enjoys an intense Mediterranean climate with mild winters and long hot summers during which rain rarely falls. Maximum temperatures reach 33°C in Aug. on the coasts and 35°C inland, with a winter minimum of 8°C on the coasts. During the months of June, July and Aug. rain falls on less than one day a month. The maximum sea temperature of 26°C occurs in Aug. and Sep. Temperatures in the mountains are appreciably lower and Troodos is snow-covered in winter. Spring is a good time to visit Cyprus before the temperature rises too high and the countryside is fresh from winter rains.

Complaints: Although there is no formal complaints procedure in tourist establishments, problems can usually be resolved by speaking to the person in charge.

Consulates:

UK – Alexander Pallis Street, Nicosia, tel: 02-473131/7.
Republic of Ireland – Flat 301, corner of Armenias Avenue and Calypso Street, Nicosia, tel: 02-499554/499805.
Australia – 4 Annis Komninis Street, 2nd Floor, corner of Stassinos Avenue, Nicosia, tel: 02-473001.
Canada – Office 2c, Julia House, 3 Them. Dervis Street, Nicosia, tel: 02-451630.
New Zealand – Via Zara 28, Rome 00198, Italy, tel: 00-396-4402928.
USA – Dositheos and Therissos Street, Lycavitos, Nicosia, tel: 02-0465151.

Crafts: The traditional needlework, often incorrectly referred to as lace, *lefkarítika*, is still practised by women on the island, especially in the village of Lefkara (see **A-Z**) from which it takes its name. Many of the traditional handicrafts are in the process of dying out, although visitors can see traditional weaving, basketwork, copperwork, pottery and woodcarving carried out at the Handicraft Centre in Athalassa Avenue, Nicosia. The centre also has a gift shop where examples of these traditional products can be bought. See **Best Buys**.

Credit Cards: See **Money**.

Crime & Theft: Cypriots are traditionally a law-abiding people and serious crime is exceedingly rare. However, the rise in tourism, increasing numbers of foreign workers and the demise of traditional village life have led to an increasing level of petty crime, although this is far lower than in Western Europe. At one time there was no need to lock cars or even one's front door in Cyprus but now such elementary precautions are advised. Money and valuables should be kept out of sight. If you are unfortunate enough to have articles or money stolen you should report the loss to the police and obtain a copy of the police report if you intend to make a claim on your insurance. If you are arrested for any reason get in touch with your consulate immediately so that they can arrange for an English-speaking lawyer to represent you. See **Consulates, Emergency Numbers, Insurance, Police.**

Conversion Chart:

Currency: The Cyprus currency is the pound (£C) divided into 100 cents. Coins in circulation are 1, 2, 5, 10 and 20 cents, while notes are in denominations of £C0.50, £C1, £C5 and £C10. The Cyprus pound is worth more than the British pound which can give the impression of prices being less than they actually are. No more than £C50 may be taken into or out of Cyprus in Cyprus currency. There is no restriction on the amount you can take into Cyprus in foreign currency or traveller's cheques and the unspent balance can be freely exported. Sums in excess of $1000 should be declared on arrival.

Customs: If you are invited to a Cypriot house you are likely to be offered a pastry or preserved fruit, a glass of water and possibly coffee. It is discourteous to refuse these but you can decline a second helping.

Customs Allowances:

Duty Free Into:	Cigarettes	*or* Cigars	*or* Tobacco	Spirits	Wine
Cyprus	200	50	250 g	0.75 *l*	1 *l*
UK	200	50	250 g	2 *l*	1 *l*

Cyprus is not a full member of the EC and therefore the lower duty-free allowances apply when returning to the UK.

Cyprus Tourism Organization: This is operated by the Cyprus Government to promote tourism. It produces a number of free publications on various aspects of travel in Cyprus as well as maps and hotel lists, and can give personal advice on how best to enjoy your holiday on the island. The staff are usually exceedingly helpful and the UK office is at 213 Regent Street, London W1R 8DA, tel: 071-7349822. There are also offices on Cyprus in Nicosia, Limassol, Larnaca, Paphos, Platres and Ayia Napa, as well as at Limassol harbour and Larnaca and Paphos airports. See **Guides**, **Opening Times**, **Tours**, **What's On**.

Disabled People: There are few facilities for the disabled on Cyprus. If you are disabled you should notify your tour operator or hotel in advance of any special requirements and remember to read the small print on insurance documents. Although most UK medicines are available on Cyprus it is sensible to take an adequate stock with you. See **Health**, **Insurance**.

KEO Vinery

Drinks: Cyprus produces a wide range of red and white wines. The best of these are produced by the major vineries which have invested in modern technology and are quite pleasant, even if nothing to excite the connoisseur, and are marketed under brand names such as Othello and Aphrodite. Although there are some good dry wines, Cyprus wines tend to be sweet and indeed one of the island's best products is the incredibly sweet dessert wine known as Commandaria, reputedly first produced by the Knights of St. John of Jerusalem. Lesser-quality wines are usually sold in large wicker-encased (or nowadays plastic-encased) flasks at remarkably low prices – usually the deposit on the flask is more than the cost of its contents! Cyprus brandy, produced in large quantities and costing from 75 cents to £C4 a bottle, is at the heart of that most Cypriot of cocktails, the brandy sour. Lower proof-strength brandies are also available and sometimes drunk with food in winter instead of wine or beer. A refreshing and popular lager is brewed by KEO (see LIMASSOL-ATTRACTIONS), the major Cyprus drinks producer, and is known simply as Keo Beer; its main rival is Carlsberg, brewed under licence in Cyprus. A number of liqueurs are produced on the island, the most popular of these being the orange-flavoured Filfar. Imported beers and spirits are available but expensive; imported wines are not widely available in Cyprus. Locally-manufactured soft drinks, as well as orange and grapefruit juices, are widely available and invariably of excellent quality. If you ask for coffee in Cyprus you will get Greek coffee served black in small cups with a glass of water. Order it *glikó* if you want it sweet, *métrio* for medium and *skéto* if you prefer it without sugar. If you want instant coffee make sure you ask for a Nescafé. Tap water in all parts of Cyprus can be drunk safely and in the mountains where it comes from springs it is usually of excellent quality. However, bottled water, both local and imported, is inexpensive and widely available.

Driving: A national driving licence or an international driving licence is required to drive in Cyprus. Green card insurance is not accepted and drivers must have insurance issued by a company officially autho-rized to transact motor insurance in Cyprus; in practice this is not a problem since few short-term visitors bring their own cars to the island.

The Cypriots drive on the left. Use of front seat safety belts is compulsory and children under ten may only sit in the front seat if a suitable child's seat belt is fitted; children under five must in no circumstances be carried in the front seat.

Speed limits are 50 kph (30 mph) in built-up areas, 100 kph (60 mph) on motorways and 60 kph (40 mph) elsewhere. There are also minimum speed limits, usually 65 kph, on most stretches of motorway. There is a motorway system linking the towns of Nicosia, Limassol and Larnaca. Otherwise there is little dual carriageway in Cyprus and slow-moving commercial traffic not only hampers progress but on occasion provokes reckless overtaking. An additional problem can be the strong sunlight, particularly when the sun is low in the sky as when travelling west in the late afternoon. It also pays to treat farm vehicles with respect as they tend to pull out onto main roads oblivious to oncoming traffic.

While the main roads between towns are of a reasonable standard, the secondary roads, particularly in the mountains, require considerable care since they are narrow with terrifying hairpins and sometimes have rough or unmetalled surfaces.

The Cyprus Government is very anxious to improve its road safety record and police patrols are common. It is therefore prudent to observe the speed limits and not drink and drive. The Breathalyzer is used as in the UK.

Town centres, particularly those of Nicosia and Limassol, are very congested and have complicated one-way systems. In general these are best explored on foot. See **Accidents & Breakdowns**, **Car Hire**, **Parking**, **Petrol**.

Drugs: Drugs are illegal and the attitude of the Cypriots is far from liberal. Those caught in possession should not expect sympathetic treatment. Contact your consulate (see **A-Z**) if you are arrested for a drugs-related offence.

Eating Out: Although not a destination for the gourmet, Cyprus has a wide variety of eating places offering competent cooking and excellent value for money. Fast-food establishments abound, ranging from steak

houses to pizzerias and burger bars. Particularly popular are establishments offering baked potatoes with a variety of toppings. Kebabs in pitta bread are a good local quick meal and usually excellent value. For a more substantial meal, tavernas and restaurants provide traditional Greek menus. Fish in Cyprus is less abundant than in Greece and tends to be expensive, and fresh seafood such as lobster is even more expensive. There are, however, a number of good fish restaurants in the coastal towns. Most Greek restaurants do not serve a wide range of desserts, the Cypriots usually favouring to eat fresh fruit after their meal. For those with a sweet tooth, patisseries – *zacharoplasteíon* in Greek – serve a range of very sweet pastries as well as delicious cakes. French cuisine is available in some of the more expensive Nicosia restaurants and some five-star hotels, and there are also a number of Chinese and some Indian restaurants on the island. The large Arab community in Limassol operates restaurants offering Lebanese dishes.

Restaurants and cafés add a 10% service charge and a 3% tax levied by the Cyprus Tourism Organization (see **A-Z**) to their charges. Sometimes this is included in the menu prices and sometimes not. When comparing prices you should take note of the establishments' policies.

Lunch or dinner for one in an inexpensive restaurant will cost £C2-4, in a moderate restaurant £C4-8 and over £C8 in an expensive restaurant. See the **RESTAURANTS** topic pages for **AYIA NAPA**, **LARNACA**, **LIMASSOL**, **NICOSIA** and **PAPHOS**, **Food**.

Electricity: The supply is 240 V 50 Hz AC and 13 amp square-pin plugs of the type used in the UK are found in most modern buildings. US appliances designed to run on 110 V supplies should not be used in Cyprus.

Emergency Numbers:

Police	199
Ambulance	199
Fire	199
Night pharmacy	192

Events:

1 January: New Year's Day. The New Year is a major celebration in Cyprus and traditionally the time, rather than Christmas, when people exchange gifts.

6 January: Epiphany. In the coastal towns the blessing of the sea takes place when the bishop throws a cross into the sea to be retrieved by one of the young men who dive in after it.

25 March: Greek Independence Day, commemorating the 1821 Greek uprising against the Turks, is celebrated by parades all over Cyprus.

1 April: EOKA Day commemorates the start of the EOKA uprising against the British in 1955.

1 May: Labour Day.

15 August: The Assumption of the Virgin is a popular day for the Cypriots to go for a picnic with the family. Roads, particularly those in the Troodos mountains, will be very congested. Many businesses close completely for a week at this time of year (although not those serving tourists).

1 October: Cyprus Independence Day, celebrated with a military parade in Nicosia.

28 October: Ochi ('No') Day commemorates Greece's rejection of Mussolini's ultimatum in 1940 and is celebrated with parades all over Cyprus.

24-25 December: Christmas, while always an important religious feast, traditionally took second place to Easter in the Cyprus calendar. Commercialization of Christmas is, however, on the increase.

Easter (movable feast): The Orthodox Easter does not always coincide with Western Easter. The fifty days of fasting before Easter is preceded by a two-week carnival with parades, fancy dress and parties. The citizens of Limassol are noted for their carnival celebrations. Easter itself is accompanied by church services throughout Holy Week, culminating in the late service on Easter Saturday preceded by a bonfire and fireworks. See **Festivities**.

Ferries: Ferry services run between Cyprus ports and Piraeus, Rhodes, Beirut, Haifa, Port Said, etc. Packaged visits to Egypt or the Holy Land are available from a number of local tour operators. It should be noted that ferry sailings are restricted in the winter months.

Festivities: A number of village festivals take place between Aug. and Sep. with folk music and dancing as well as exhibitions of agricultural produce and handicrafts. There is also a Nicosia festival in June and a folklore festival in Limassol in May. The Limassol wine festival at the end of Aug. is a popular event among Cypriots and visitors alike, while for beer drinkers there is the Carlsberg festival held at the Carlsberg brewery south of Nicosia at the beginning of July. Since dates may vary from year to year it is best to contact the Cyprus Tourism Organization (see **A-Z**), which can give full details of all the above as well as conferences and sporting events. See **Events**.

Food: Cyprus food is essentially that found in Greece and Turkey and throughout the eastern Mediterranean. There are, however, some Cyprus specialities worth trying, including ewe's-milk cheese, *halloúmi*, usually served toasted, and smoked pork, *loúnza*. Other typically Greek/Cyprus dishes include:
Souvlákia: Cubes of meat, either lamb or more commonly pork, grilled on a skewer over a charcoal fire.

Sheftaliá: Meatballs seasoned with herbs and cooked over charcoal.

Keftédhes: Spicy meatballs fried in oil.

Mezés: A meal composed of numerous small dishes, usually starting with bread and a selection of dips, followed by fish and meat dishes and ending with a selection of charcoal-grilled meats.

Dolmádes: Vine leaves stuffed with a mince-rice mixture and cooked in the oven.

Kléftiko: Lamb sealed in a container and slowly cooked in an oven until the meat falls off the bone.

Afélia: Pork cooked in wine and coriander.

Stifádo: A beef and onion stew.

Barboúnia: Red mullet, usually grilled over charcoal.

Lithríni: Grey mullet, usually grilled over charcoal.

Synagrída: Akin to sea bass, this much-prized fish is expensive but delicious when charcoal-grilled.

Soupiá: Cuttlefish either deep-fried or grilled whole over charcoal.

Tavás: Pieces of lamb, potato and tomato cooked slowly in the oven.

Kalamári: Squid cut into rings, battered and deep-fried.

Talatoúri: A dip containing cucumber, garlic and yoghurt, known in Greece as *tzatziki.*

Taramosaláta: A dip of fish roe, cream, olive oil and spices.

Tashí: A dip made from sesame seed paste, lemon juice and garlic, know in Greece as *tahini.*

Spinakópita: Spinach in a pastry casing – a common Cyprus snack.

Tirópita: Another Cyprus snack, this time with cheese in a pastry case.

See the **RESTAURANTS** topic pages for **AYIA NAPA, LARNACA, LIMASSOL, NICOSIA** and **PAPHOS, Eating Out.**

Guides: Trained and licensed guides can be obtained through the Cyprus Tourist Guides Association, PO Box 1942, Nicosia, tel: 02-457755. A list of qualified guides is also obtainable from the Cyprus Tourism Organization (see **A-Z**). Approximate charges are £C20 for half a day and £C30 for a full day. An appreciable surcharge may be made on Sun. and public holidays (see **A-Z**). See **Tours**.

Health: There are no particular health problems in Cyprus and standards of hygiene in hotels and restaurants are generally good. There are able doctors and dentists in all the major towns, many trained in Britain; most doctors indicate where they qualified on the signs outside their surgeries, making it easy to select a British-trained doctor who therefore has a knowledge of English. Hospital facilities are adequate. Unlike Britain you may consult a specialist directly without first obtaining a letter of referral from a general practitioner.

Most doctors will expect payment in cash at the end of a consultation; however, fees are usually reasonable. Receipts should be obtained for doctors fees and medicines if you intend to make an insurance claim. Cyprus has reciprocal arrangements with Britain on health care, details of which can be obtained from your local DSS office. Nevertheless it is highly advisable to take out a private health insurance policy to cover both cost of treatment and emergency repatriation in case of accident or serious injury.

If you intend to take part in any sporting activities that could be classified as hazardous, read the small print of your policy carefully since these may be excluded.

Hospital telephone numbers:

Nicosia General Hospital	tel: 02-451111
Limassol General Hospital	tel: 05-330333
Larnaca General Hospital	tel: 04-630311
Paphos General Hospital	tel: 06-232364
Paralimni Hospital	tel: 03-821211
Polis Hospital	tel: 06-321431
Kyperounta Hospital	tel: 05-532021

See **Chemists**, **Disabled People**, **Emergency Numbers**, **Insurance**.

Insurance: You should take out a travel insurance policy which covers you against theft and loss of property and money, as well as medical expenses, for the full duration of your stay. Your travel agent should be able to recommend something suitable. See **Crime & Theft**, **Driving**, **Health**.

Language: Most Cypriots you will encounter are Greek-speaking, the 18% of the population of Turkish origin living mainly in the Turkish-occupied zone. Nevertheless certain official documents appear in Turkish as well as Greek. English is taught in all schools and you will find it widely understood, especially in establishments catering for tourists. However, if you can manage a few words in Greek you will find it greatly appreciated. Despite its unfamiliar alphabet it is not difficult to pick up a few basic greetings from a good Greek phrase book (see the Collins *Greek Phrase Book & Dictionary*), although it is important to pay attention to your pronunciation since you will only be understood if you stress words correctly.

Those who already speak some Greek will have no difficulty in towns or with radio and television but may face problems in the more remote villages and rural areas where a very heavy dialect is commonly spoken. If this happens to you it may be some consolation that Greeks from the mainland sometimes experience the same difficulty.

Problems can also arise from transliteration of Greek place names since there is no standard system of transliteration and it is possible to be confronted with several variations such as Agia Napa, Aghia Napa and Ayia Napa or Paphos and Pafos. This is further complicated in that some places have Anglicized names rather different from the Greek, for example Nicosia which in Greek is pronounced Lefkosía, Leukosia or Levcosia (depending on the system of transliteration employed). A further example is Limassol from the Greek form Lemesós.

Laundries: Launderette facilities are not widely available although some hotels offer a laundry service. In summer washing will dry quickly on your hotel balcony. Dry-cleaning services are available in all towns.

Lost Property: If you lose anything do not give up – the Cypriots are an honest people. If you can remember where you lost the article, go back and see if anyone has kept it for you; otherwise contact the police. If you intend to claim for a loss on your insurance it will be necessary to obtain a certificate from the police. See **Insurance**.

Markets: The visitor may notice the relative rarity of greengrocers, butchers and fishmongers in Cyprus towns. This is because many Cypriots still prefer to buy fresh produce from the markets which are open daily (except Sun.). Most markets also have stalls selling handicrafts such as basketwork and are lively bustling places as smallholders come in from the countryside to sell their produce. They are well worth a visit, preferably in the morning, even if you do not wish to buy. See **Best Buys**, **Crafts**.

Money: All the towns have branches of the major banks, including the Bank of Cyprus, the Cyprus Popular Bank and the National Bank of Greece, as well as the international divisions of European banks such as Barclays. In tourist areas some banks remain open outside normal hours (0830-1200) for foreign exchange dealings. Money can also be exchanged in hotels although the rate is usually less favourable. You will need your passport when exchanging currency or cashing traveller's cheques. Credit cards and Eurocheques are quite widely accepted, particularly at more up-market establishments, although their use is by no means as widespread as in the UK. Away from the tourist areas it is always advisable to carry sufficient cash for all your anticipated needs. See **Crime & Theft**, **Currency**.

Museums: The principal archaeological collection in Cyprus is housed in the Cyprus Museum (see **NICOSIA-ATTRACTIONS 1**) and covers the period from the Neolithic age to early Byzantium. Folk art of the 19th and 20thC can be seen in the Folk Art Museum in the old Archbishopric in Nicosia, which also houses the Byzantine Museum and art galleries (see **NICOSIA-ATTRACTIONS 1**). The towns of Limassol, Larnaca and Paphos all have their own archaeological museums. The Pierides Museum (see **LARNACA-ATTRACTIONS 1**) also contains an important private archaeological collection. Opening hours vary according to season and can be checked locally with the Cyprus Tourism Organization (see **A-Z**).

Music: Musical tastes in Cyprus mirror those of Greece, with bouzouki music (a long-necked, plucked string instrument resembling a large mandolin) being popular, together with British and American pop music, particularly among the young. The strange tones of traditional Cyprus dance music are occasionally heard on the radio and can also be heard at Cyprus evenings in hotels and restaurants.

Newspapers: English and other foreign newspapers are widely available, usually the day after publication. The English-language *Cyprus Mail* carries local and a limited amount of international news. *Cyprus Weekly*, with feature articles and information, as well as *Cyprus Time Out,* is published in English. See **What's On**.

Nightlife: In contrast to the mainland Greeks the Cypriots in general are not night owls. However, this does not prevent the discos in the tourist areas opening until the early hours. Admission to a disco,

including one drink, will cost £C3-4 (moderate) and £C5 or more in an expensive establishment. More traditional entertainment may be had at a *bouzoukia* listening to soulful songs sung to a bouzouki (see **Music**) orchestra accompaniment but be warned, such establishments are not cheap. Displays of folk dancing are sometimes organized by hotels and restaurants. The few remaining cinemas (video rentals having caused most to close), sometimes open-air in summer, show Greek, European and American films. The latter are invariably subtitled rather than dubbed so may be of interest to the visitor. Expect to pay £C1.50 for a ticket. However, many visitors simply enjoy lingering over a meal or a drink in a café. See the NIGHTLIFE topic pages for AYIA NAPA, LARNACA, LIMASSOL and PAPHOS, **Opening Times**.

Noise: Cypriots believe in accompanying every activity with the maximum amount of noise, whether blaring music, shouting or car horns. If you are likely to be disturbed by this make sure you ask for accommodation away from main roads.

Nudism: Topless bathing is common and tolerated on most beaches and in many hotel pools on Cyprus. Nudity, however, is illegal and, unlike some beaches in Greece, a blind eye is not turned to it.

Opening Times: Opening times are subject to variation and should be checked locally. Currently summer opening hours apply during the period 1 May-30 Sep. Tourist facilities tend to open when there are customers about and may have restricted opening hours during off peak periods. Some tourist facilities close in winter. Discos and nightclubs generally open around 2100, get fully underway by midnight and close in the early hours, though times tend to reflect demand.

Cyprus Tourism Organization (see **A-Z**) offices in Cyprus open every morning (except Sun.) and on Mon. and Thu. afternoons.

Shops (winter) – 0730-1400 Mon.-Fri., 0730-1300 Sat.

Shops (summer) – 0730-1330 Mon.-Sat.

Shops selling tourist items may open outside these hours.

Public services (winter) – 0730-1400 Mon.-Fri., 0730-1300 Sat.

Public services (summer) – 0730-1330 Mon.-Sat.

Banks – 0830-1200 Mon.-Sat. Some branches offer afternoon tourist services on weekdays.

Orientation: Cyprus is the third-largest island in the Mediterranean (after Sicily and Sardinia). Its capital is Nicosia and it is divided into six administrative districts: Famagusta, Kyrenia, Larnaca, Limassol, Nicosia and Paphos. The whole of the Kyrenia district and part of the Famagusta, Larnaca and Nicosia districts lie within the Turkish-occupied zone.

Detailed road maps (not always up to date) are readily available on Cyprus but it may be a good idea to obtain one before you go to the island in order to plan your itinerary. The Cyprus Tourism Organization (see **A-Z**) in London may be able to supply a suitable map if you cannot find one locally.

When making your plans you should bear in mind that while major roads are of an acceptable standard many of the minor roads marked on maps, particularly in the mountain areas, are little more than tracks and are best not attempted at night or in bad weather (see **Driving**). The only crossing point into the Turkish-occupied zone is in Nicosia and there are restrictions on travellers visiting the northern part of the island which should be checked locally (see **Northern Cyprus**). On no account should any attempt at illegal crossings be made; not only would you run a high risk of arrest but you could be shot at or encounter minefields! The chances of inadvertently crossing the border are remote but care should be taken if walking cross-country in the vicinity of the Green Line (see **A-Z**), though this activity is not recommended. You will see the names of places that lie in the Turkish-occupied zone on road signs in the South; this does not mean you can actually drive to them.

City plans can be obtained from branches of the Cyprus Tourism Organization. Make sure any plan you use is up to date as renaming streets is a Greek national sport.

In Greek house numbers follow the street name. It is usual to omit the word for 'street' (*odhós*), thus Omirou 7 translates as '7 Homer Street'. You may also encounter the Greek terms *leofóros* and *platía* meaning 'avenue' and 'square' respectively; these are not omitted.

Parking: Other than in the centres of the major towns, particularly Nicosia and Limassol, parking is not a problem. In urban areas there are meters and car parks, the latter charging approximately 30 cents per half day. As in Britain you may not park on double yellow lines. Parking restrictions are strictly enforced by wardens and fines. There are car parks in Nicosia in the moat of the walled city and in Limassol on the promenade opposite the town centre. See **Driving**.

Passports & Customs: A valid passport is required for a stay of up to three months. No visa is required for UK citizens. Persons entering Cyprus through ports or airports in the Turkish-occupied part of the island as well as those with Turkish Cypriot visas in their passports will not be granted entry to territory controlled by the Republic of Cyprus. You may bring into or take out of Cyprus up to £C50 in Cyprus currency. There is no limit on the amount of foreign currency or traveller's cheques you may bring in although amounts in excess of US$1000 must be declared on entry on form D(NR). Exchange thus imported and declared may be re-exported on departure. See **Customs Allowances**.

Petrol: This is sold by the litre and is relatively inexpensive compared with most of Europe. Most petrol stations are attendant-operated. There are few rural petrol stations. Most petrol stations open 0600-1800 Mon.-Fri. On Sat. and Sun. they open on a rota basis from 0600-1600. Some have automatic pumps operated by inserting a banknote. If you are motoring late in the evening or over the weekend it is advisable to maintain a full tank. Unleaded petrol is not yet in widespread use. See **Driving**.

Police: The police wear khaki uniforms with navy blue caps in summer and navy blue uniforms in winter. Almost all policemen speak some English and are usually helpful. See **Crime & Theft**, **Emergency Numbers**.

Post Offices: These can be found in all major towns. However, stamps can be obtained more conveniently from one of the numerous kiosks to be found all over the island as well as from hotels. Post offices open 0730-1330 (1300 in summer) Mon.-Sat.; some offer afternoon services. Note that telegrams cannot be sent from post offices; for these you should go to the offices of the Cyprus Telecommunications Authority (CYTA) (see **Telephones & Telegrams**).

Public Holidays: 1 Jan. (New Year's Day); 6 Jan. (Epiphany); Clean Mon. (variable – 1st Mon. of lent 50 days before Greek Orthodox Easter); 25 Mar. (Greek Independence Day); 1 April (EOKA Day); Good Fri. (variable); Easter Sat. (variable); Easter Mon. (variable); 1 May (Labour Day); 15 Aug. (Assumption); 1 Oct. (Cyprus Independence Day); 28 Oct. (Ochi Day); 25 Dec. (Christmas Day); 26 Dec. (Boxing Day). Greek Orthodox Easter does not always coincide with the date of Easter as celebrated in Western Europe.

Rabies: Although uncommon it is a good idea to take the precaution of having all animal bites seen to by a doctor.

Religious Services: Although the population is predominantly Greek Orthodox there are Anglican and Roman Catholic churches in Larnaca, Limassol, Nicosia and Paphos. Details of services can be obtained from the Cyprus Tourism Organization (see **A-Z**).

Shopping: See **Best Buys**, **Markets**.

Smoking: Traditionally Cypriots have been heavy smokers although nowadays anti-smoking campaigns are having some effect. Nevertheless, there are few restrictions on smoking in public places other than on buses and in taxis.

Sovereign Base Areas: Under the treaty through which Cyprus gained its independence from Britain, the UK retained 256 sq. km of land to be used for military bases known as Sovereign Base Areas. The major of these are Akrotiri-Episkopi (RAF) in the south and Dhekelia (Army) in the southeast. Main roads run through both of these and you have a right of way to use them, although it is possible there may be security checks. The Sovereign Base Areas have their own police who enforce traffic regulations very strictly.

Sports:

Active sports:

Fishing: There is no restriction on sea fishing with a rod. A licence is required for spear fishing with an aqualung which certified divers may obtain by application to the fisheries department in

Larnaca, Limassol or Paphos. Fishing for a number of species including trout and carp is permitted at certain dams. A licence is required which can be bought at the district fisheries departments, from whom further details may be obtained.

Tennis: There are tennis clubs in the major towns and some of the larger hotels have their own courts.

Horse riding: There are riding centres in Limassol and Paphos and at Deftera, 11 km from Nicosia.

Diving: There are diving schools at all coastal towns and in addition some hotels provide diving facilities.

Water sports: A wide range of water sports, including water skiing, windsurfing and paragliding, is available at all popular beaches. You should not drive speedboats within the red buoys indicating bathing areas.

Hiking: The Troodos mountains (see **A-Z**) offer excellent opportunities for hikers. There are four marked trails on Troodos and a leaflet giving details of these together with the wildlife likely to be encountered can be obtained from the Cyprus Tourism Organization (see **A-Z**).

Skiing: There are several ski lifts in the Troodos area although the season is short, usually Jan. through to the beginning of Mar.

Spectator sports:

Horse racing: There is a flat course in the Nicosia suburb of Ayios Dhometios with regular meetings except July-mid Sep.

Rallying: The 72 hr Cyprus Rally is a major event that takes place in Sep.

Football: A semi-professional soccer league plays in winter.

Taxis: These can be recognized by an illuminated sign on their roof; their registration numbers also start with the letter T. Most are metered and are plentiful and relatively cheap (a typical fare is Larnaca–Nicosia, 47 km, approximately £C12). Shared service taxis run between major towns and are good value (Larnaca–Nicosia £C1.50). These will pick you up and drop you off anywhere within the central area. All you need do is telephone the taxi office about an hour before you wish to travel and tell them where to collect you. For a small group of people a taxi can be a good way of touring the island; many taxi offices display rates for such excursions. See **Tipping**.

Telephones & Telegrams: Cyprus has a modern internationally-connected STD telephone system. Local and international calls can be made from call boxes, some of which take phonecards available from posts offices, kiosks and souvenir shops (£C2 and £C5). Telegrams can be sent by telephone during weekdays, tel: 196, and from offices of the Cyprus Telecommunications Authority (CYTA). Most telephone operators speak good English.

To telephone abroad dial 00 followed by the code for the country (UK – 44, USA – 1, Ireland – 353), the UK STD code without the initial zero and the number you require.

Directory Enquiries   (local)   192
                        (international)   194

Television & Radio: The Cyprus Broadcasting Corporation Radio Programme 2 (603 KHz) broadcasts news, weather and details of cultural events in English, Turkish, Arabic and Armenian, as well as light and classical music. The British Forces Broadcasting Service broadcasts in English 24 hr a day. You should also be able to pick up the BBC World Service.
Television broadcasts contain a number of British and American series which are subtitled in Greek. There are also daily news bulletins in English.

Time Difference: 2 hr ahead of GMT in winter and 2 hr ahead of BST in summer. However, the days on which the clocks change in Cyprus and the UK do not usually coincide.

Tipping: Service charges are included in hotel and restaurant bills (see **Eating Out**) but a modest tip will be appreciated if the service is of a good standard. Tipping of taxi drivers is optional and should not be more than 10% of the fare. Porters in hotels should be tipped about 50 cents.

Toilets: There are a few public toilets in the larger towns but it is wise to use the facilities in restaurants and cafés. Tourist beaches run by the Cyprus Tourism Organization (see **A-Z**) have good toilet facilities.

Tourist Information: See **Cyprus Tourism Organization**.

Tours: A number of companies run a selection of guided bus tours and these offer an alternative for the visitor who does not wish to drive. Sea tours are also available to both Israel and Egypt. Detailed information can be obtained from any travel agent in Cyprus. See **Guides**.

Transport: Buses, while offering a reasonable service within towns, are not to be recommended for travel between towns. Service taxis offer a speedier and more comfortable means of transport with door-to-door service yet at a modest cost. Without doubt hiring a car is the best way to explore the island in detail. However, if you don't like driving, many taxi drivers offer fixed-priced excursions which can be tailor-made and are not too expensive, particularly if you can get together with others to share the cost. Motorcycles and mopeds can also be hired but should be driven with care since they are prone to accidents on the uneven Cyprus roads. When planning travel in Cyprus you should remember that roads, particularly those in the mountains, are not up to British standards and you should allow for this in estimating journey times. Although it is technically possible to fly from Larnaca to Paphos, distances in Cyprus are not great enough to warrant domestic air travel. There is no railway on Cyprus. A number of boat trips operate in summer between points on the coast. See **Airports**, **Buses**, **Ferries**, **Taxis**.

Traveller's Cheques: See **Money**.

Water Sports: See **Sports**.

What's On: The Cyprus Tourism Organization (see **A-Z**) publishes a number of lists of cultural events which may be obtained free from its offices. They will also be able to give you details of events such as the Limassol carnival and Limassol wine festival. *Cyprus Time Out* carries details of entertainments, shopping, etc. Listings of cinemas, duty chemists, etc. can be found in the English-language *Cyprus Mail*. See **Events**, **Festivities**, **Newspapers**.

Youth Hostels: There are youth hostels in Nicosia, Limassol, Larnaca, Paphos and Troodos open to members of the International Youth Hostels Association. Details can be obtained from the Cyprus Youth Hostel Association, PO Box 1328, Nicosia.

Panayia Angeloktistos, Kiti

This edition published 1997 by Diamond Books
77-85 Fulham Palace Road, Hammersmith,
London W6 8JB

Text: Niki Watts
Photography: Monica Wells
Electronic Cartography: Bartholomews

First published 1993
Copyright © HarperCollins*Publishers*

Printed in Italy by Amadeus S.p.A.

ISBN 0 261 66901-X